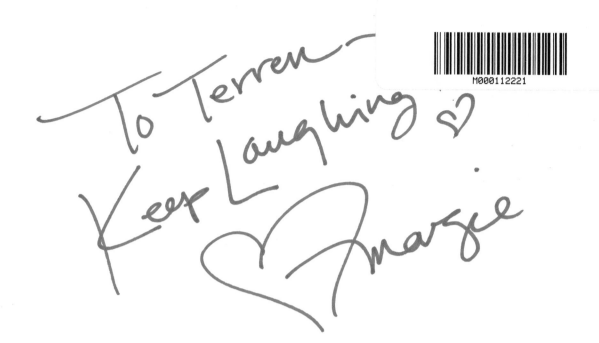

To Terren—
Keep Laughing ♡
♥ Margie

To mothers everywhere…
But especially my own,
Malvina Cherry

Book design by HumorOutcasts Press.

Published 2016 by HumorOutcasts Press
Printed in the United States of America

ISBN: 0-998-08990-7
EAN-13: 978-099808990-4

# ACKNOWLEDGEMENTS

Thanks to the peeps who made this possible:
- ♥ Ivan Kimmelman & Ken Kauffman for technical assistance on a gargantuan scale
- ♥ Mike McGurl for his cover design patience
- ♥ Carol Sabik Jaffe for helping to make it happen
- ♥ Donna Cavanagh for her booklife-midwife skills
- ♥ Sasha & Dana Kimmelman for allowing me to turn their lives into material
- ♥ Ivan for making me a mother and making it all possible

# INTRODUCTION

Twenty-five years ago, when I had been drawing "The Art of Motherhood" for a year, I looked at my black-and-white cartoons and thought,

> "Wouldn't these make a really fun coloring book for moms? Moms could color away in their own special book while their kids were coloring in theirs!"

Everyone I mentioned this idea to thought I was out of my mind. "Why in the world would grownups want to color?" they said incredulously. I dropped the idea.

♥

So now that adult coloring books are all the rage, I revisited my original idea to bring you this, "Mom's Comedy Coloring Book…'Cuz Why Should Our Kids Have All the Fun?"

But I wanted MY coloring book to be different- not only relaxing, but fun, entertaining, creative, energizing, and even empowering!

♥

Most adult coloring books just promise to zone you out.

THIS coloring book takes that relax-you-factor and adds LAUGHTER, with its cocktail of happy chemicals (like dopamine and endorphins) to boost your mood and your immune system, AND mixes in a healthy dose of CREATIVITY to flex your brain and re-energize you with the adrenaline-rush of creating your own comedy. Relax, laugh, create. It's like sipping a glass of Chardonnay AND doing shots of espresso at the same time!

♥

Based on my long-running cartoon "The Art of Motherhood", one of the first cartoons to skewer the saintly image of mothering, you'll laugh out loud while coloring in cookie jars and cranky kids…but that's not all.

You'll get a shot at cartooning-it-yourself on our exclusive CIY pages to stretch your creative muscles and turn your OWN frustrations into funnies!

And for those of you who crave a bigger canvas, we've also included three Big Coloring Pages (BCP) so you can cover a lot of territory with your 64 (or more) colors.

Enjoy!

♥

# INSTRUCTIONS

Instructions for a coloring book? C'mon.... YOU know what to do!
Grab your favorite markers or pencils, dive in, and get gloriously ga-ga while you giggle! Feel free to add your own elements and punch lines and don't worry about staying inside the lines. This book is meant to make you happy, so do whatever the heck you want with it. Go crazy! Laugh outside the lines!

But what you MIGHT need a little help with is creating your own cartoons on the CIY pages. Here's how to Cartoon-it-Yourself (CIY):

- Use the cartoon that comes before each CIY page as a clue. For example:
    - "Hip 'N Helpful Accessories for Middle-Aged Moms" shows a mom's hands tattooed with reminders. The BCP (Big Coloring Page) after that is "The Only Tattoos We'll Let Our Children Get". The CIY that follows asks you to design your own tattoo. Obviously, you'll use this page to design a tattoo. But, don't just draw a pretty tattoo...

- Each of your cartoons should start with a problem or frustration you are experiencing:
    - What's driving you crazy about parenting, school, work, meal-time...in other words, your daily life? What is frustrating you (I know, but just choose ONE thing for now)? Is your child's early morning whining driving you to later-morning "wining"? What is making your life difficult or challenging, be it infants (little babies), partners (big babies), or all-around work-life wackiness?
    - Whatever your aggravations may be, USE THEM! It's grist for the comedy mill.
    - EXAMPLE: You have two kids and they are both driving you crazy. Your partner is lobbying hard for baby #3, and you can't imagine ever having another child

- Come up with a funny or snarky solution to the problem using the cartoon prompt
    - EXAMPLE: In the case of the tattoo, you might draw a close up of your bikini area, and just above the panty line draw a flowery tattoo with the saying "Just say NO" in flowing letters....or whatever YOUR reaction to the situation might be!

- Remember: Comedy is Problem + Solution. Humor starts with a problem, the solution is the comedy!
- Turning your frustrations into funnies is EMPOWERING!

You have power over your problems when you control them through comedy!

# Mom-servations

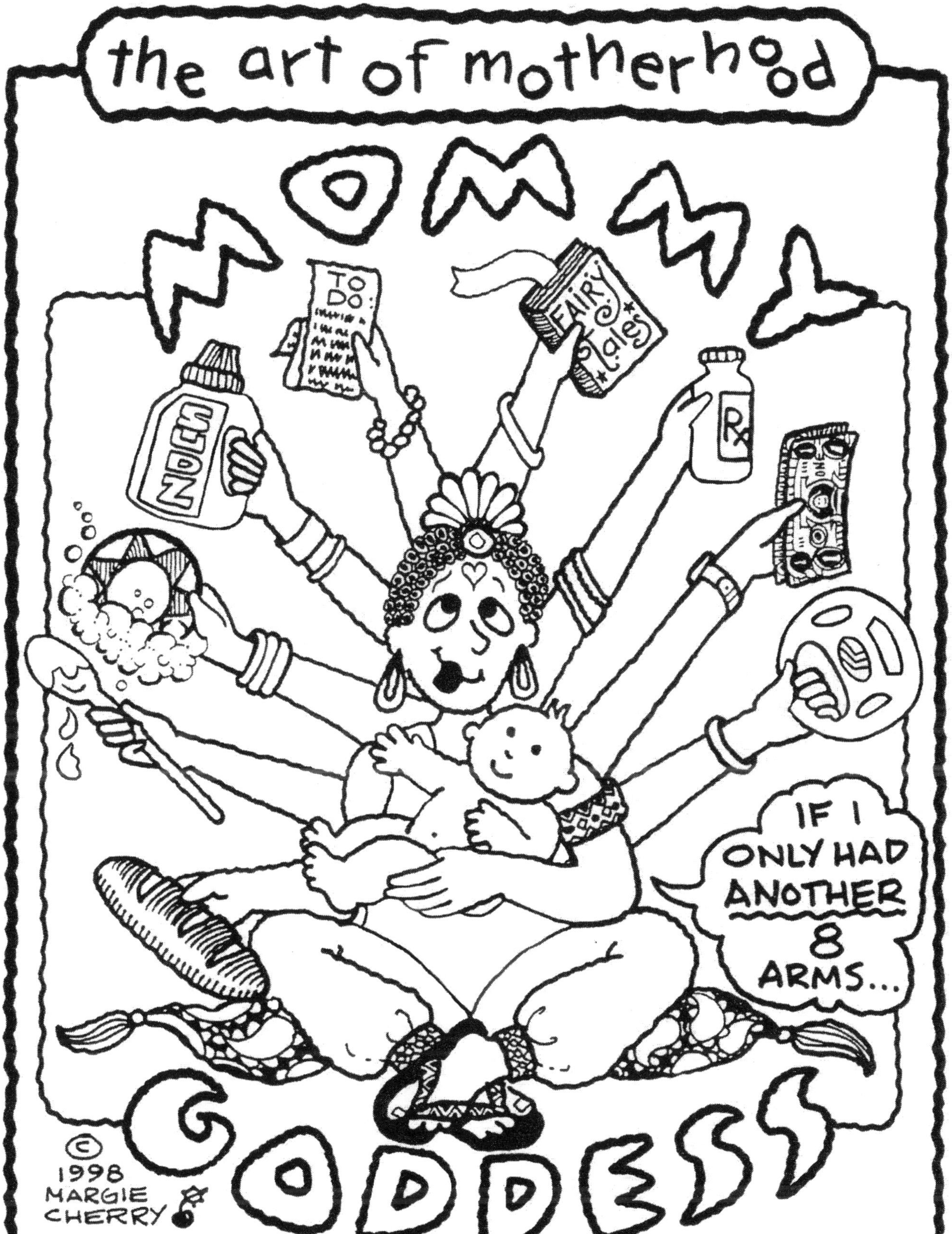
the art of motherhood
MOMMY
TO DO:
FAIRY Tales
SUDS
Rx
IF I ONLY HAD ANOTHER 8 ARMS...
GODDESS
© 1998 MARGIE CHERRY

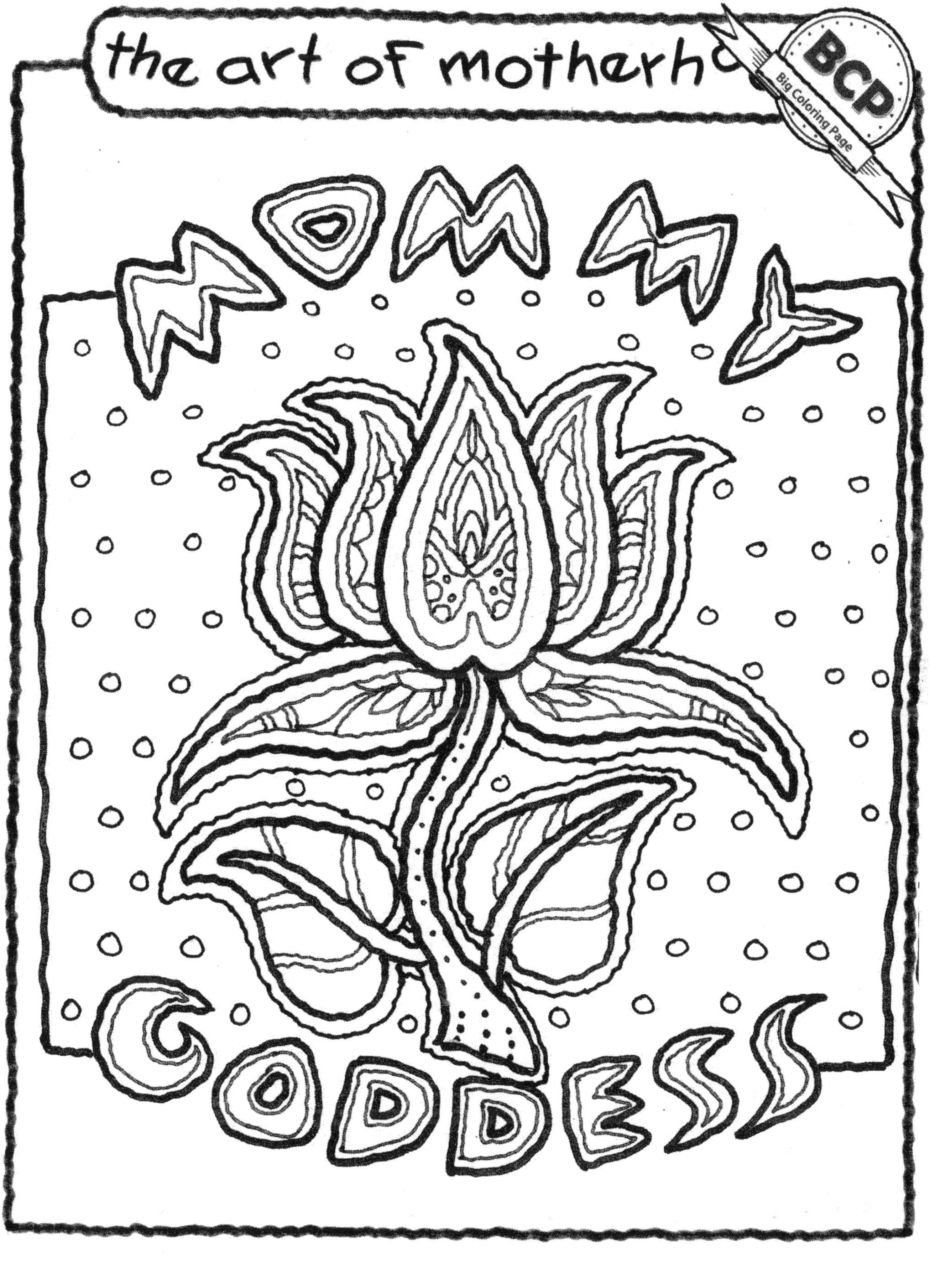
the art of motherho
BCP
Big Coloring Page
GODDESS

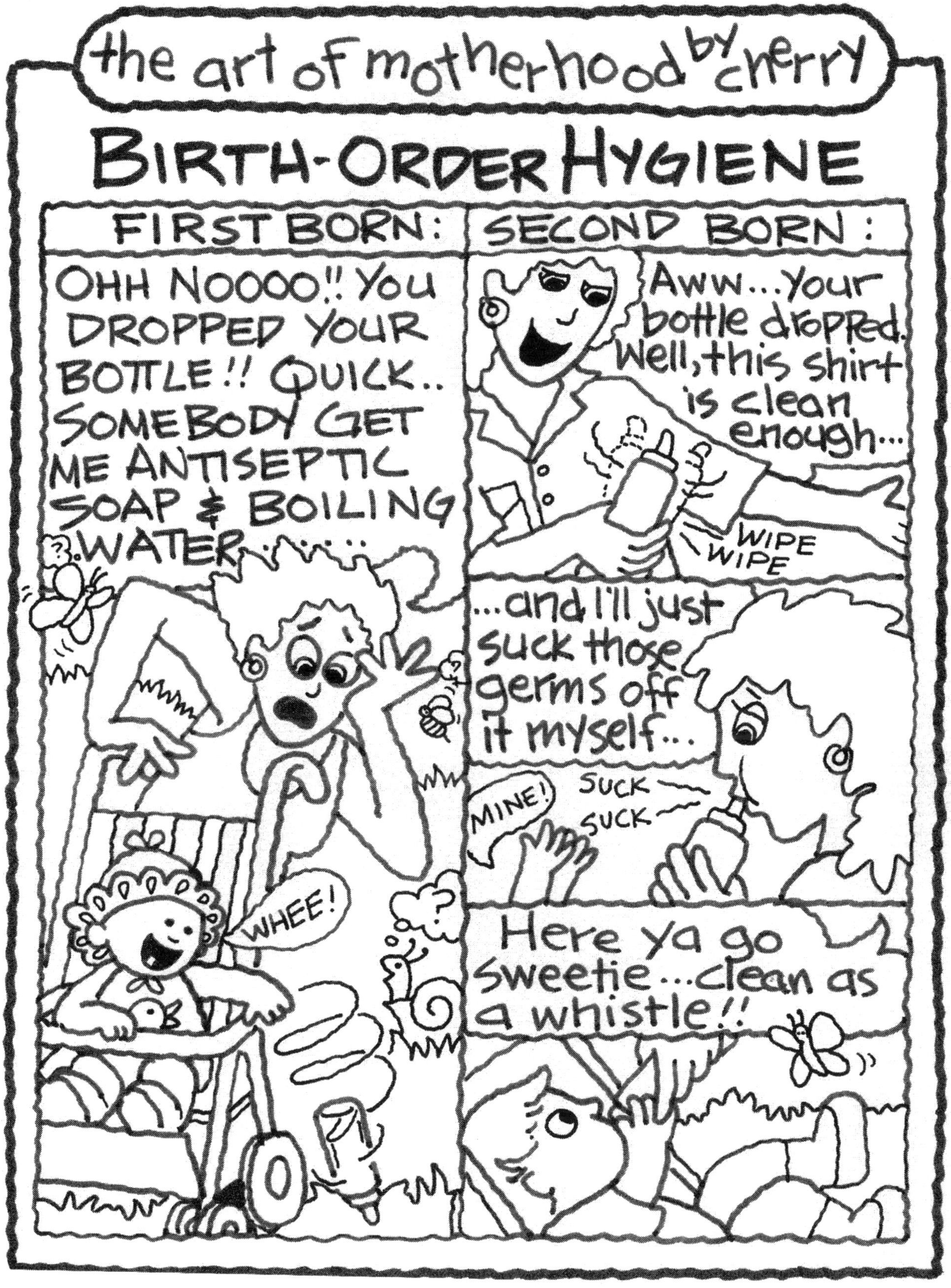
the art of motherhood by cherry
BIRTH-ORDER HYGIENE
FIRST BORN:
OHH NOOOO!! YOU DROPPED YOUR BOTTLE!! QUICK.. SOMEBODY GET ME ANTISEPTIC SOAP & BOILING WATER.......
WHEE!
SECOND BORN:
Aww...your bottle dropped. Well, this shirt is clean enough...
WIPE WIPE
...and I'll just suck those germs off it myself...
SUCK SUCK
MINE!
Here ya go sweetie...clean as a whistle!!

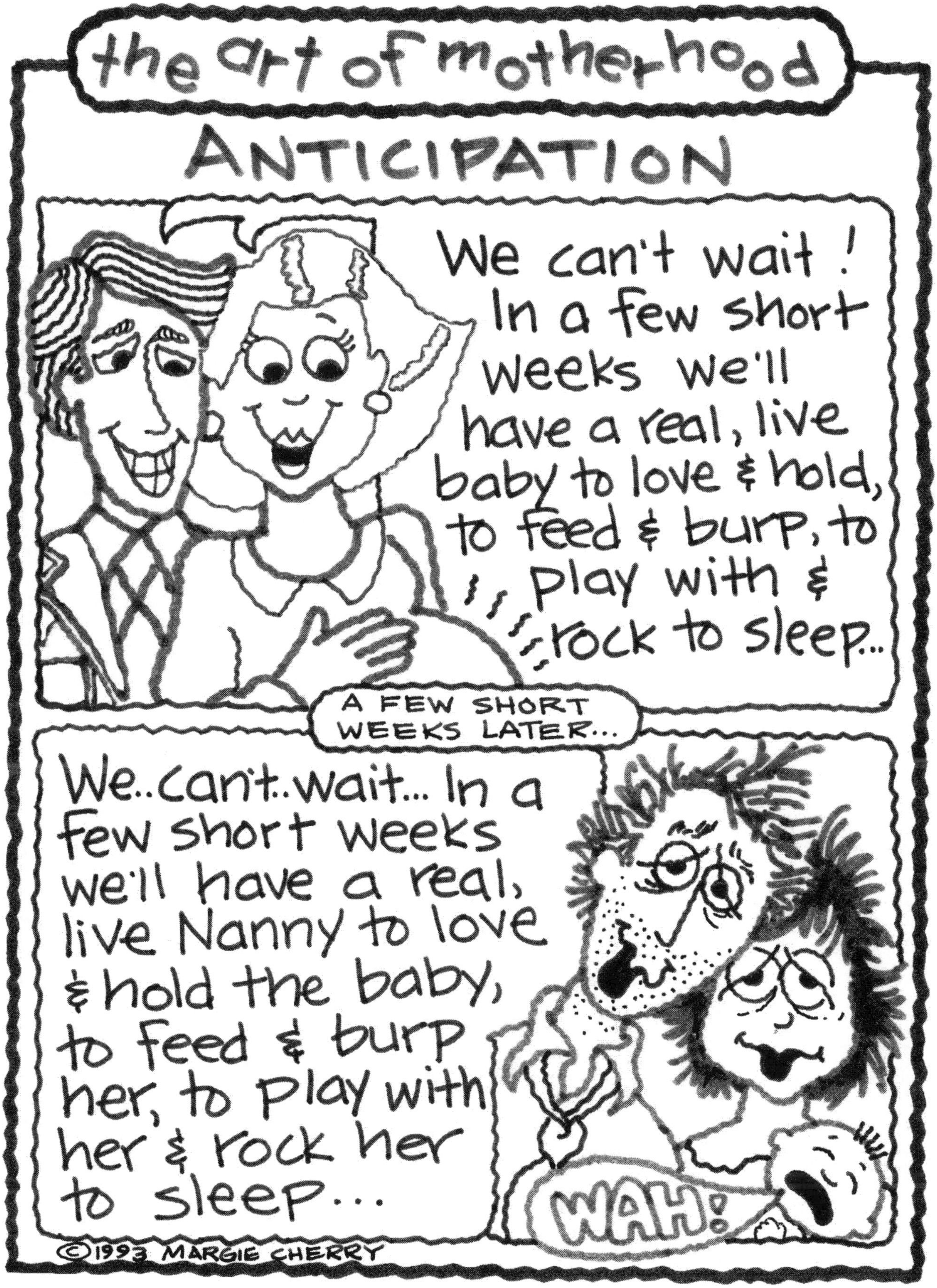

the art of motherhood
ANTICIPATION
We can't wait ! In a few short weeks we'll have a real, live baby to love & hold, to feed & burp, to play with & rock to sleep...
A FEW SHORT WEEKS LATER...
We..can't..wait... In a few short weeks we'll have a real, live Nanny to love & hold the baby, to feed & burp her, to play with her & rock her to sleep...
WAH!
©1993 MARGIE CHERRY

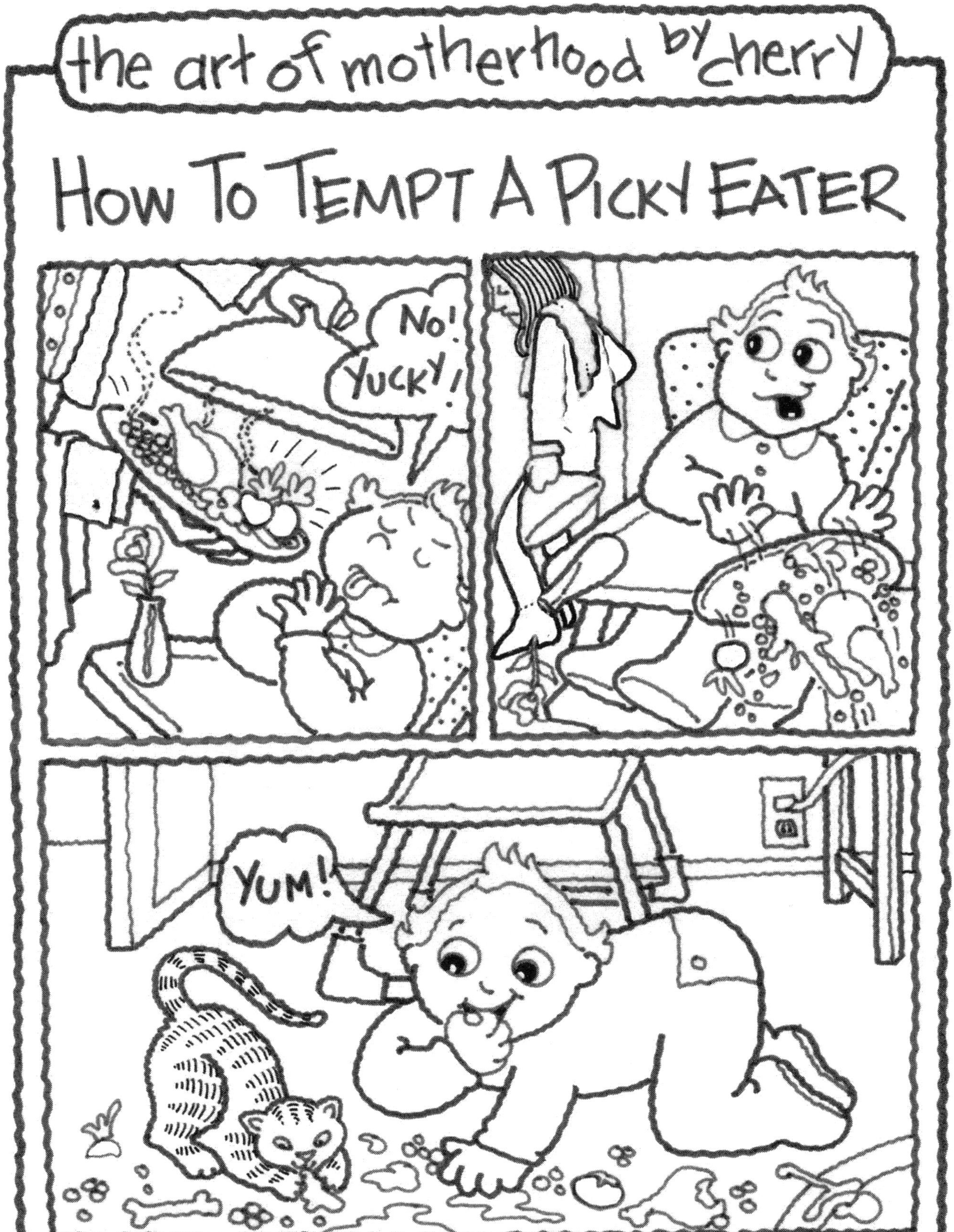
the art of motherhood by cherry
HOW TO TEMPT A PICKY EATER
NO! YUCKY!
YUM!
© 1993 MARGIE CHERRY

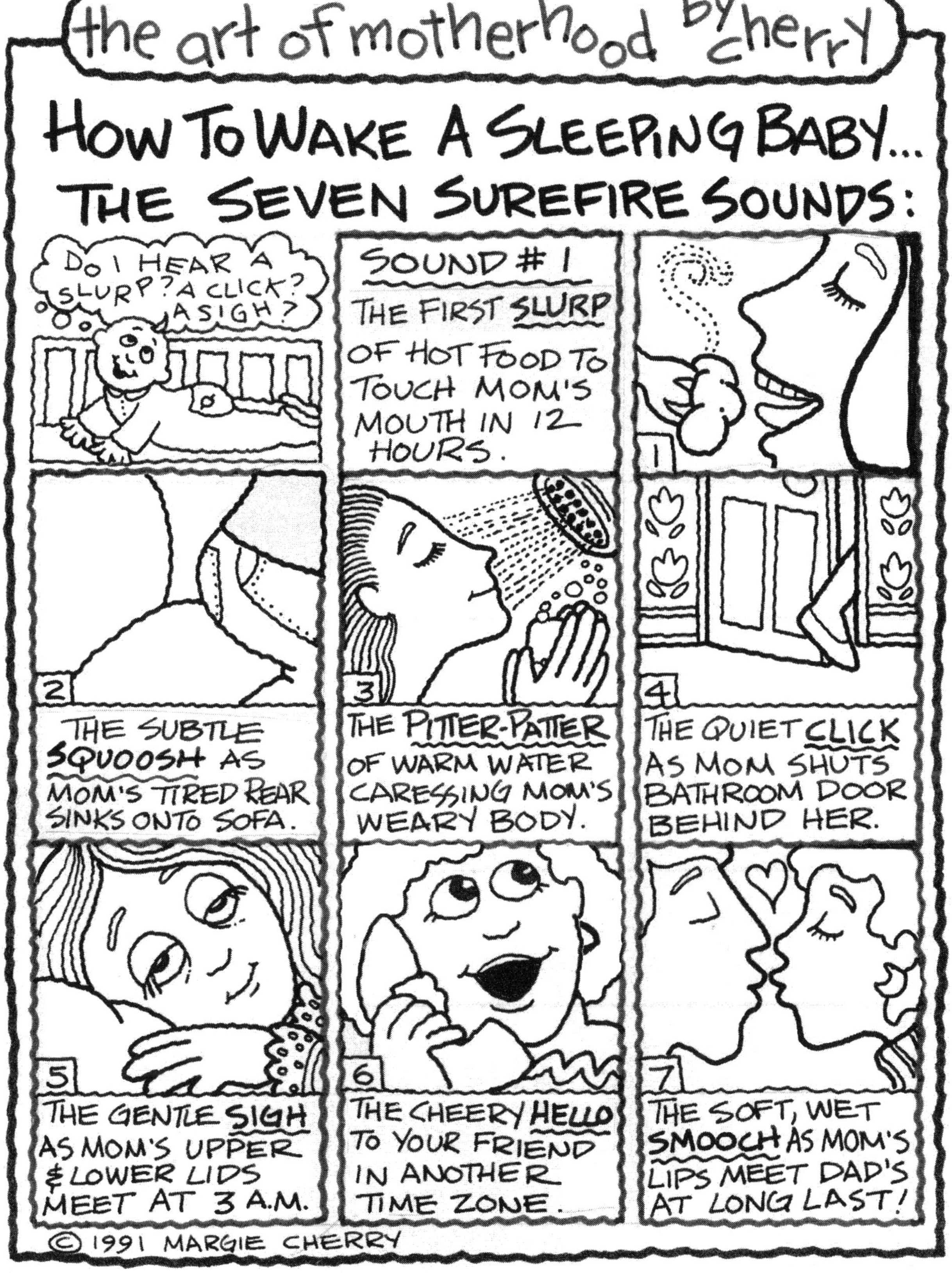
the art of motherhood by cherry
HOW TO WAKE A SLEEPING BABY...
THE SEVEN SUREFIRE SOUNDS:
DO I HEAR A SLURP? A CLICK? A SIGH?
SOUND # 1
THE FIRST SLURP OF HOT FOOD TO TOUCH MOM'S MOUTH IN 12 HOURS.
1
2
THE SUBTLE SQUOOSH AS MOM'S TIRED REAR SINKS ONTO SOFA.
3
THE PITTER-PATTER OF WARM WATER CARESSING MOM'S WEARY BODY.
4
THE QUIET CLICK AS MOM SHUTS BATHROOM DOOR BEHIND HER.
5
THE GENTLE SIGH AS MOM'S UPPER & LOWER LIDS MEET AT 3 A.M.
6
THE CHEERY HELLO TO YOUR FRIEND IN ANOTHER TIME ZONE.
7
THE SOFT, WET SMOOCH AS MOM'S LIPS MEET DAD'S AT LONG LAST!
© 1991 MARGIE CHERRY

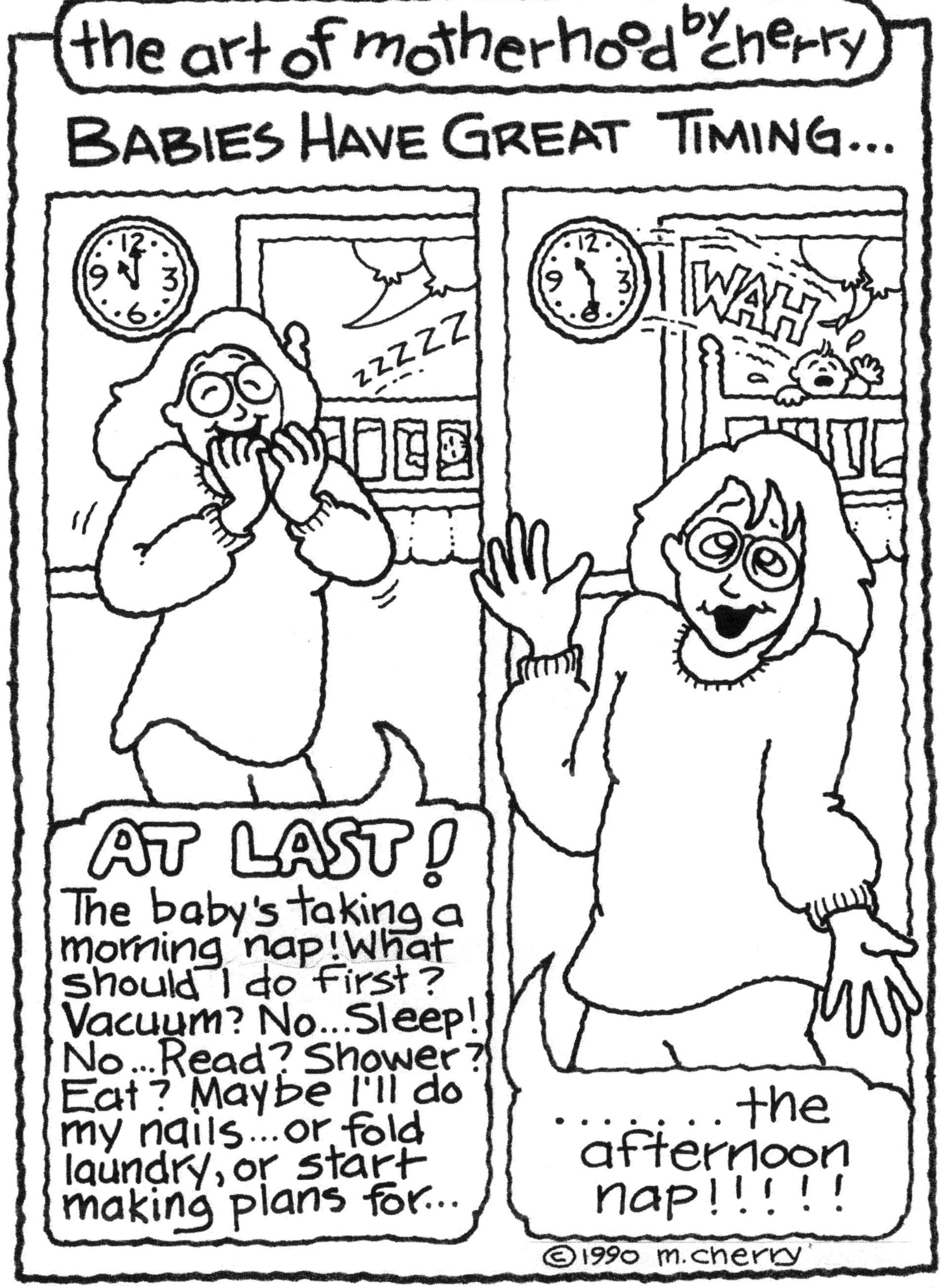

the art of motherhood by cherry
BABIES HAVE GREAT TIMING...
zzzzzz
AT LAST!
The baby's taking a morning nap! What should I do first? Vacuum? No...Sleep! No...Read? Shower? Eat? Maybe I'll do my nails...or fold laundry, or start making plans for...
WAH
.......the afternoon nap!!!!!
©1990 m.cherry

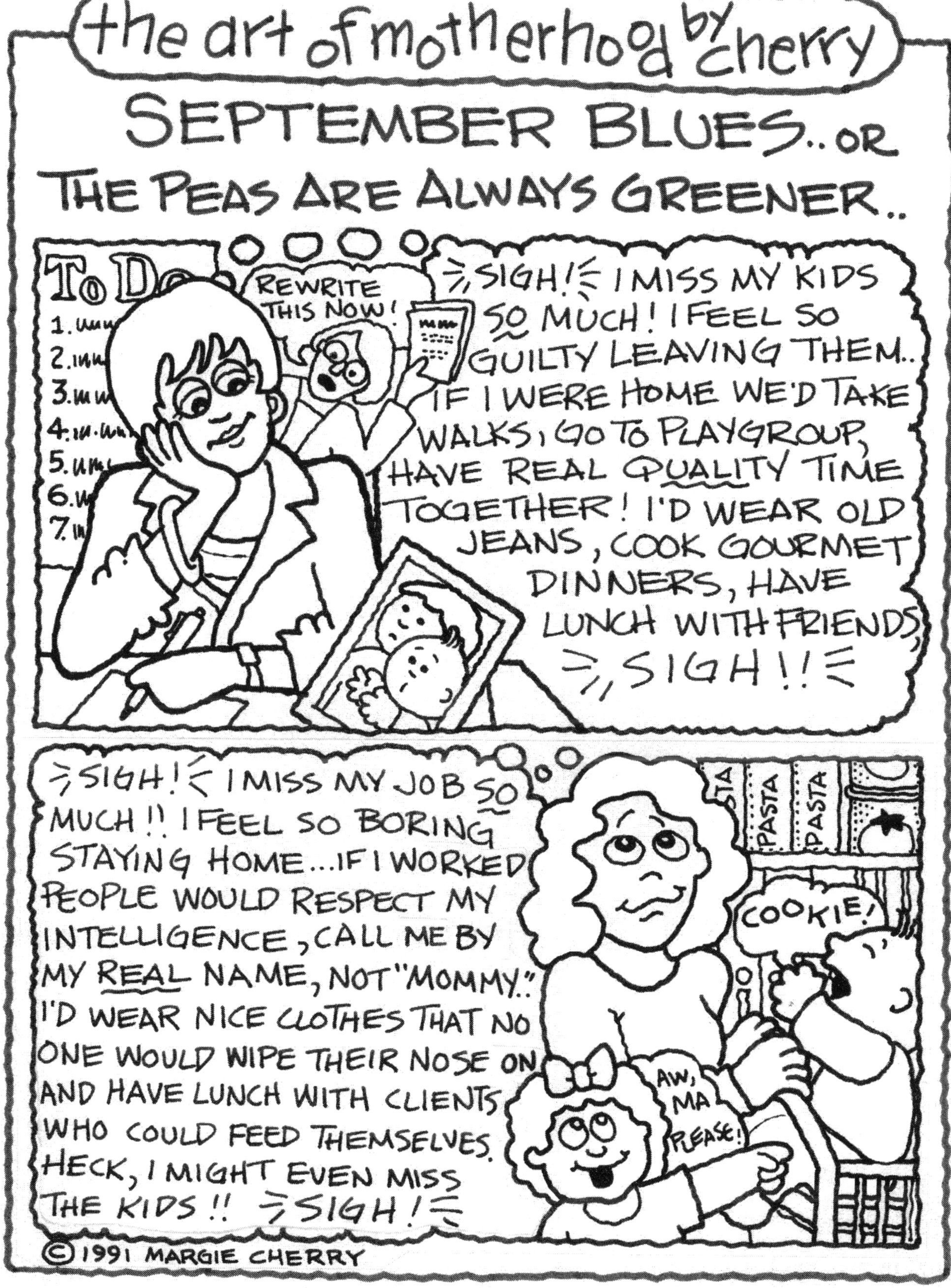
the art of motherhood by cherry
SEPTEMBER BLUES.. OR
THE PEAS ARE ALWAYS GREENER..
TO DO
1.
2.
3.
4.
5.
6.
7.
REWRITE THIS NOW!
SIGH! I MISS MY KIDS SO MUCH! I FEEL SO GUILTY LEAVING THEM.. IF I WERE HOME WE'D TAKE WALKS, GO TO PLAYGROUP, HAVE REAL QUALITY TIME TOGETHER! I'D WEAR OLD JEANS, COOK GOURMET DINNERS, HAVE LUNCH WITH FRIENDS, SIGH!!
SIGH! I MISS MY JOB SO MUCH!! I FEEL SO BORING STAYING HOME...IF I WORKED PEOPLE WOULD RESPECT MY INTELLIGENCE, CALL ME BY MY REAL NAME, NOT "MOMMY." I'D WEAR NICE CLOTHES THAT NO ONE WOULD WIPE THEIR NOSE ON AND HAVE LUNCH WITH CLIENTS WHO COULD FEED THEMSELVES. HECK, I MIGHT EVEN MISS THE KIDS!! SIGH!
PASTA
PASTA
COOKIE!
AW, MA PLEASE!
© 1991 MARGIE CHERRY

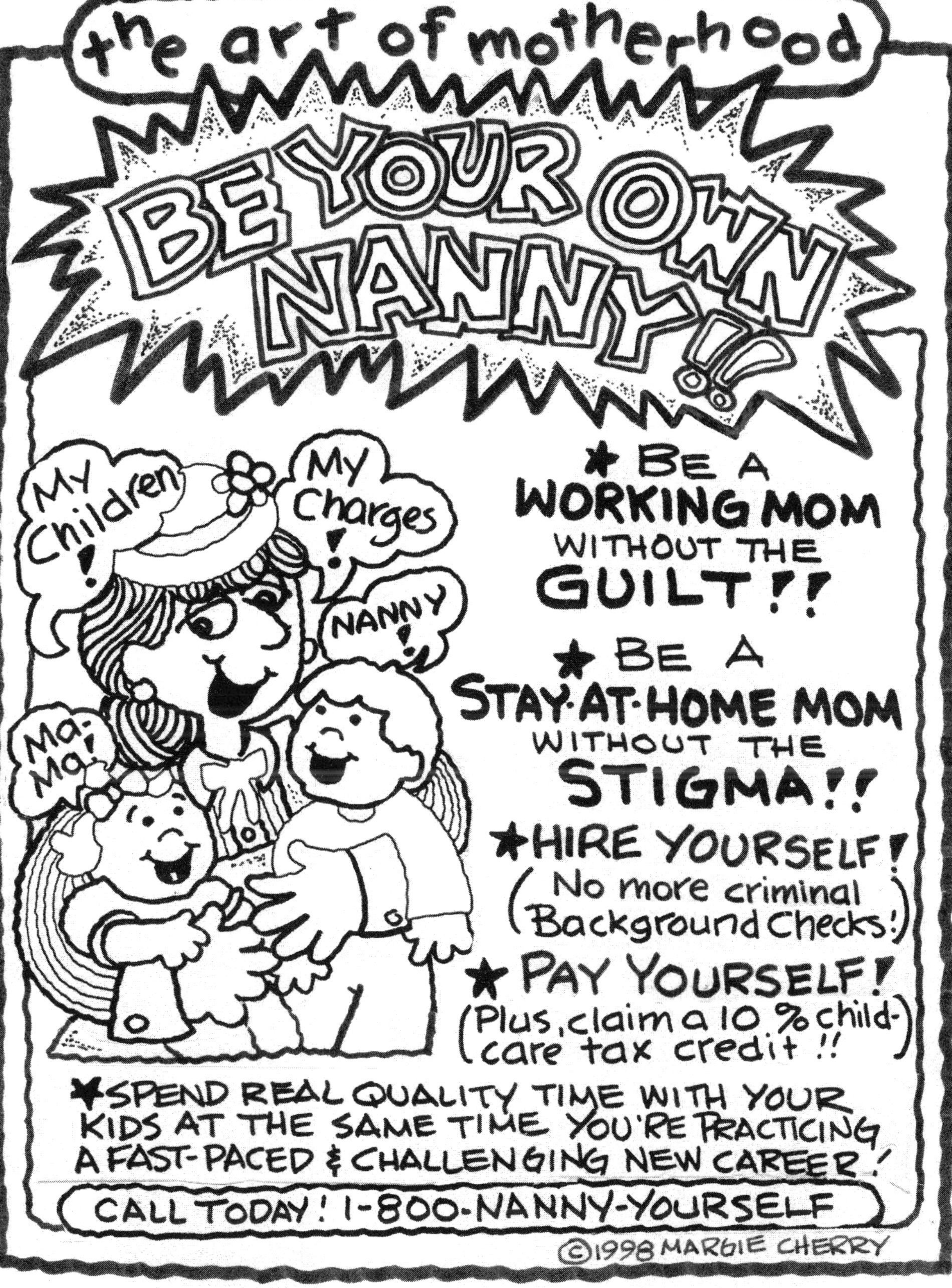
the art of motherhood
BE YOUR OWN NANNY!!
My Children!
My Charges!
NANNY!
Ma-Ma!
★ BE A WORKING MOM WITHOUT THE GUILT!!
★ BE A STAY-AT-HOME MOM WITHOUT THE STIGMA!!
★ HIRE YOURSELF! (No more criminal Background Checks!)
★ PAY YOURSELF! (Plus, claim a 10 % child-care tax credit !!)
★ SPEND REAL QUALITY TIME WITH YOUR KIDS AT THE SAME TIME YOU'RE PRACTICING A FAST-PACED & CHALLENGING NEW CAREER!
CALL TODAY! 1-800-NANNY-YOURSELF
©1998 MARGIE CHERRY

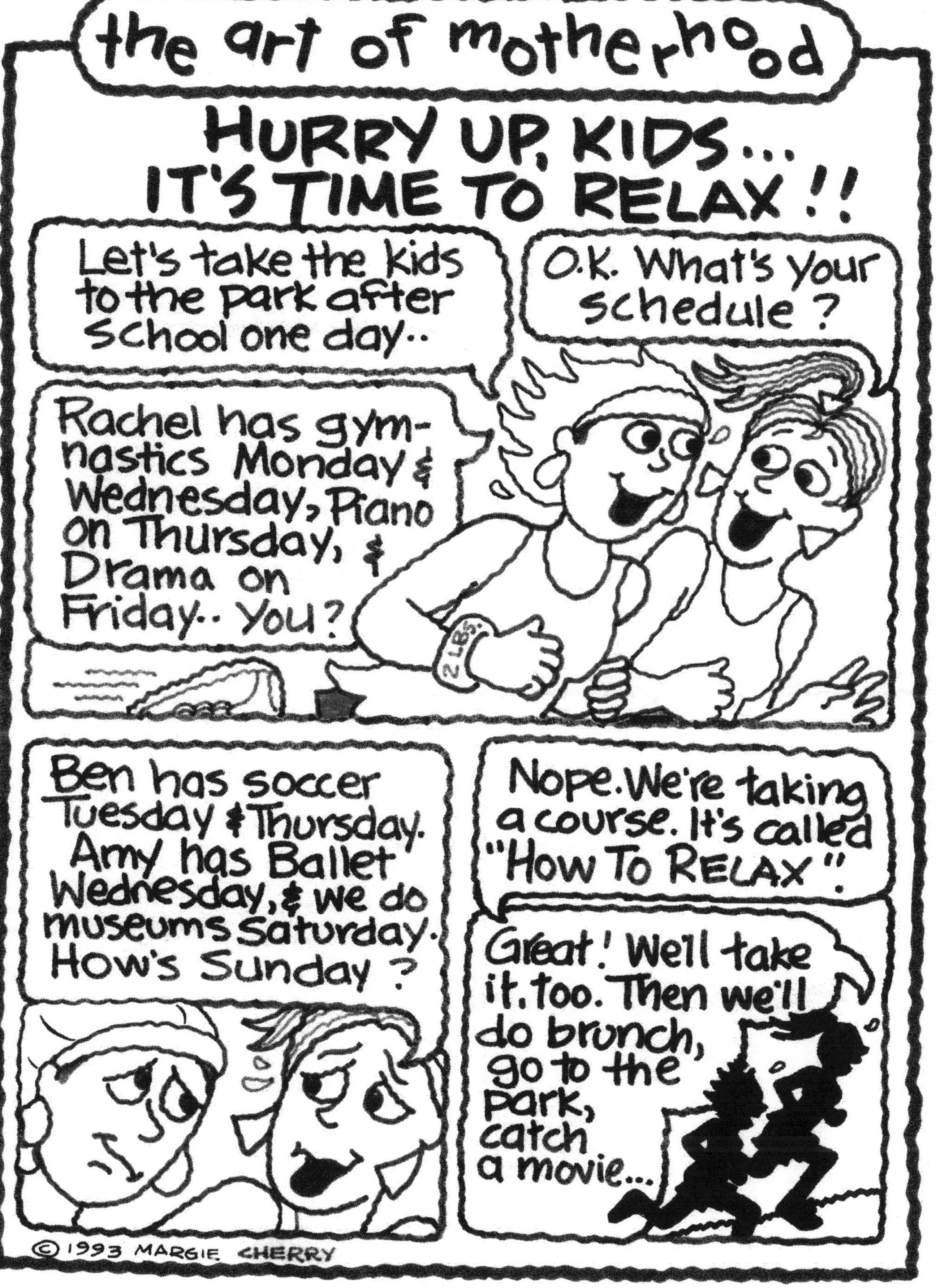
the art of motherhood
HURRY UP, KIDS... IT'S TIME TO RELAX!!
Let's take the kids to the park after school one day..
O.K. What's your schedule?
Rachel has gymnastics Monday & Wednesday, Piano on Thursday, & Drama on Friday.. You?
2 LBS.
Ben has soccer Tuesday & Thursday. Amy has Ballet Wednesday, & we do museums Saturday. How's Sunday?
Nope. We're taking a course. It's called "How To Relax".
Great! We'll take it, too. Then we'll do brunch, go to the park, catch a movie...
© 1993 MARGIE CHERRY

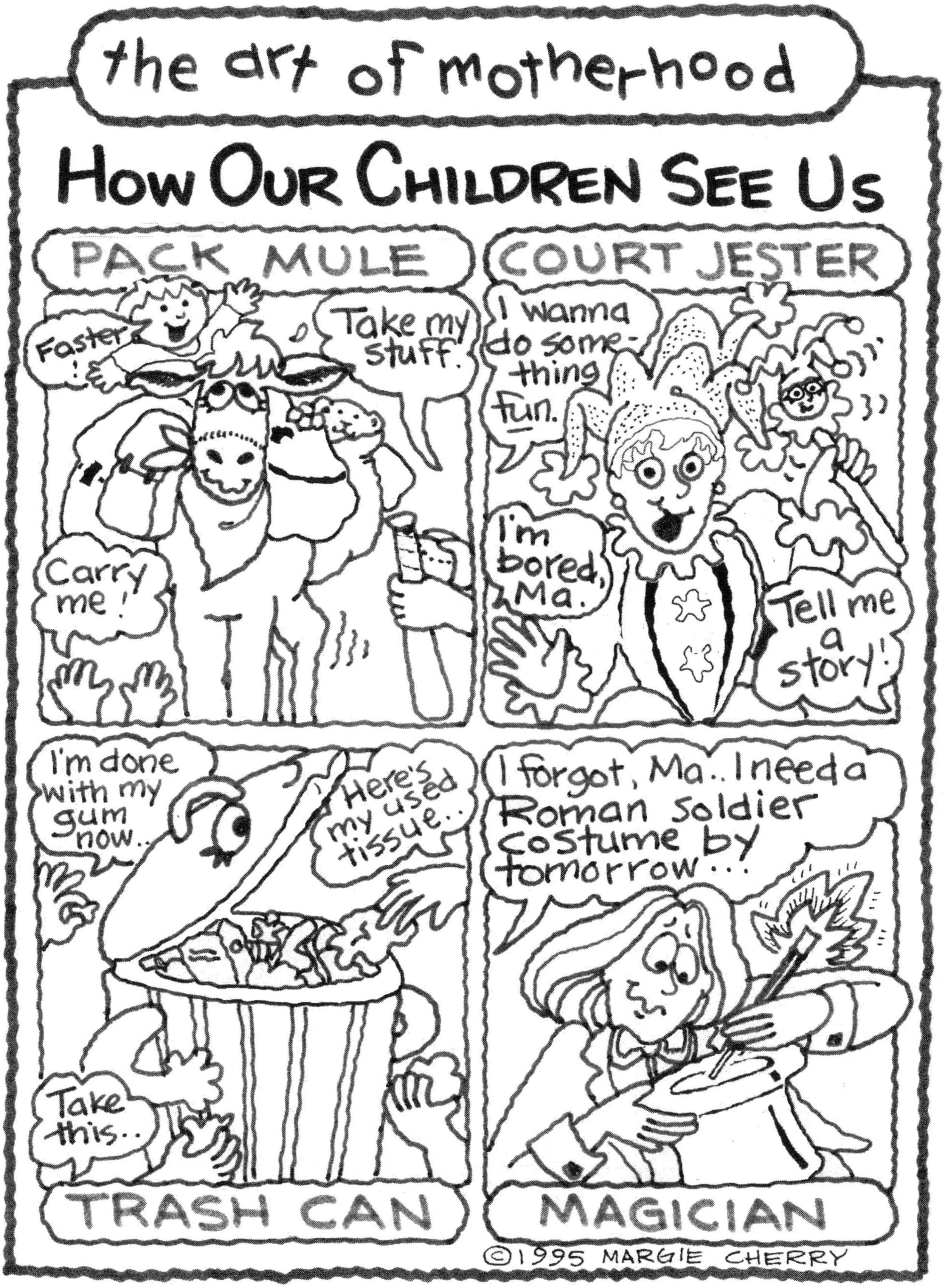
the art of motherhood
How Our Children See Us
PACK MULE
Faster!
Take my stuff.
Carry me!
COURT JESTER
I wanna do something fun.
I'm bored, Ma.
Tell me a story!
I'm done with my gum now..
Here's my used tissue..
Take this..
TRASH CAN
I forgot, Ma.. I need a Roman soldier costume by tomorrow...
MAGICIAN
©1995 MARGIE CHERRY

the art of motherh[ood]

CIY
Cartoon-It-Yourself

HOW YOUR KIDS SEE YOU

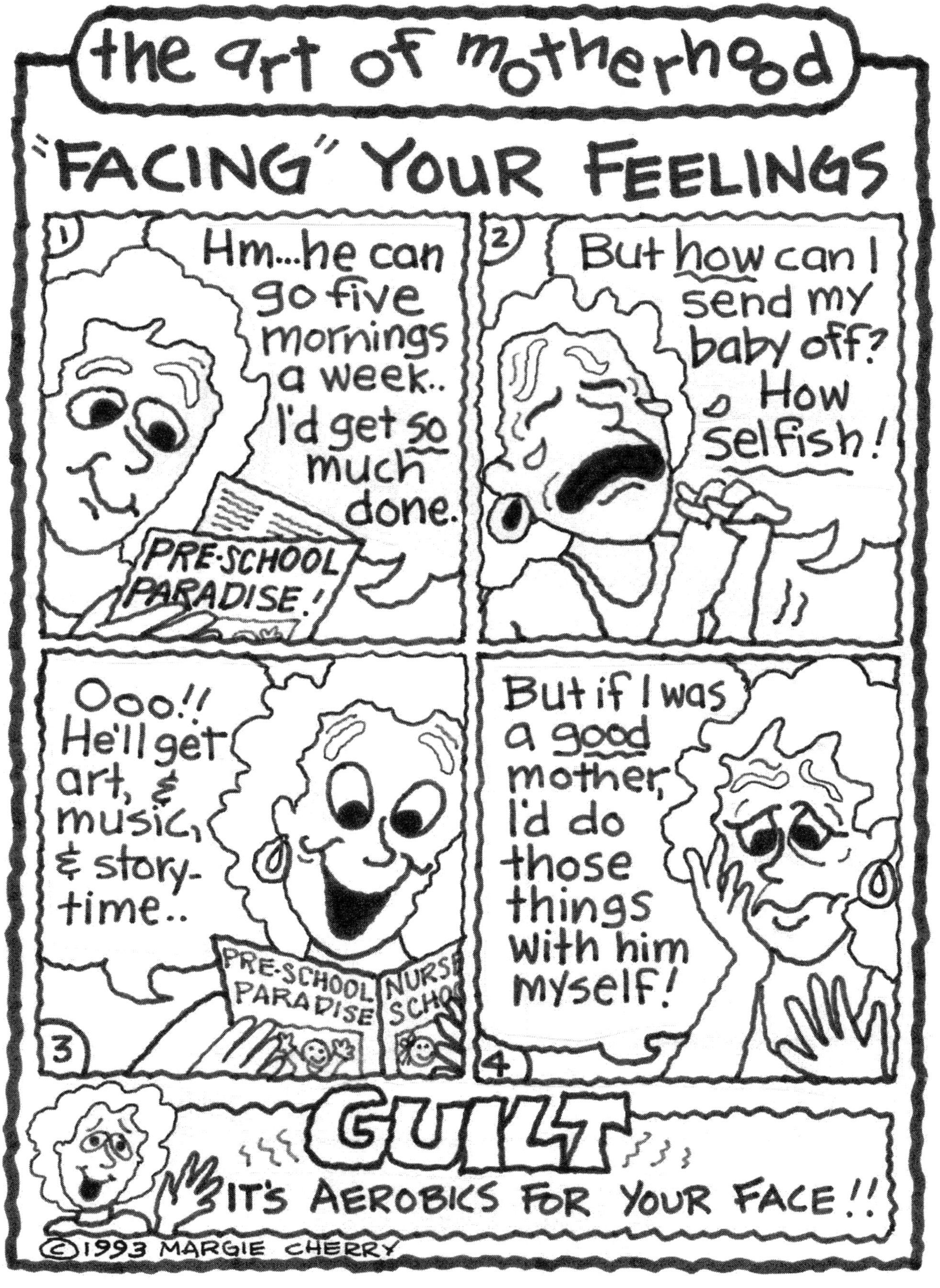
the art of motherhood
"FACING" YOUR FEELINGS
1
Hm...he can go five mornings a week.. I'd get so much done.
PRE-SCHOOL PARADISE!
2
But how can I send my baby off? How selfish!
3
Ooo!! He'll get art, & music, & story-time..
PRE-SCHOOL PARADISE
NURS SCHO
4
But if I was a good mother, I'd do those things with him myself!
GUILT
IT'S AEROBICS FOR YOUR FACE!!
©1993 MARGIE CHERRY

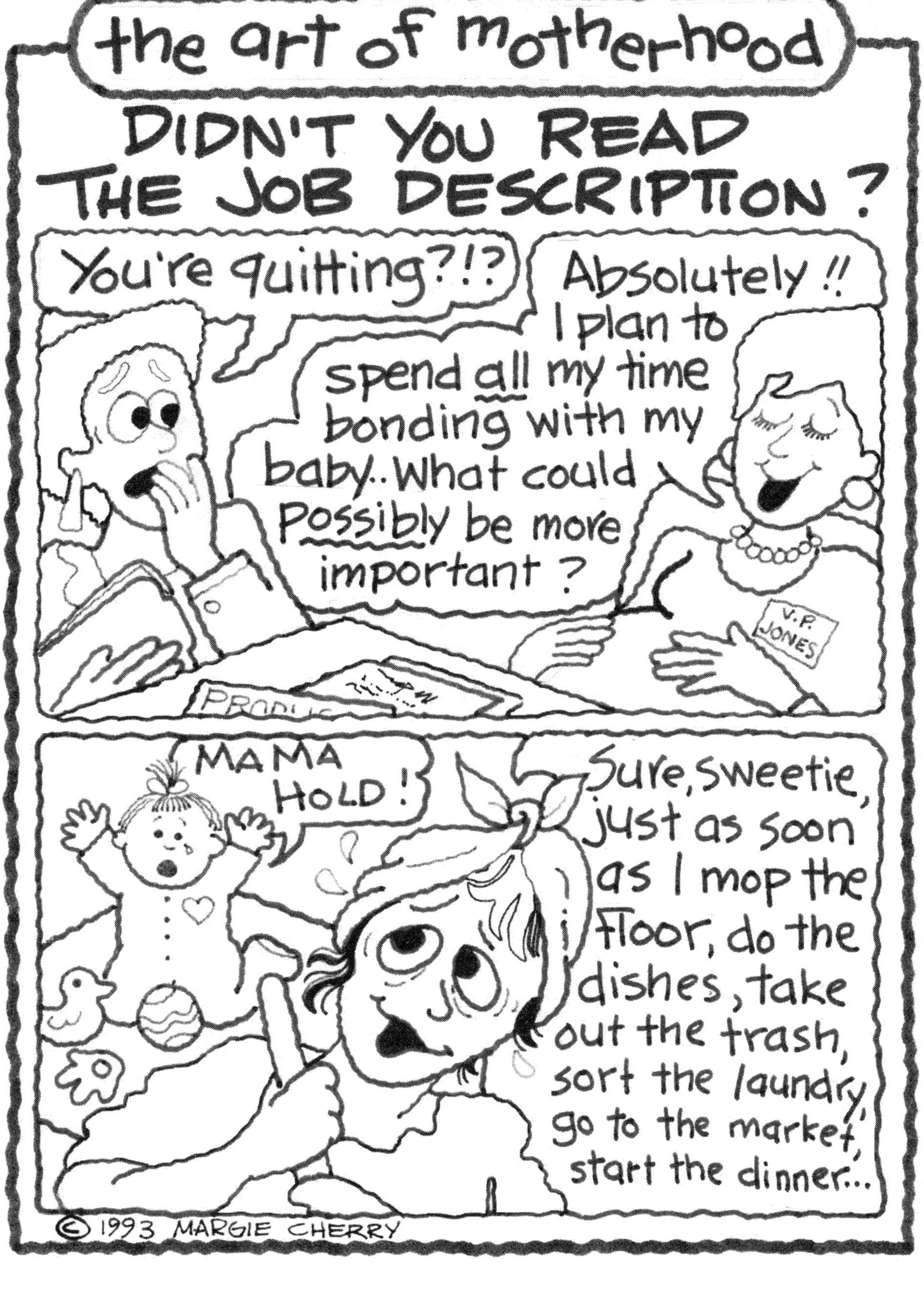

the art of motherhood
DIDN'T YOU READ THE JOB DESCRIPTION?
You're quitting?!?
Absolutely!! I plan to spend all my time bonding with my baby.. What could possibly be more important?
V.P. JONES
MAMA HOLD!
Sure, sweetie, just as soon as I mop the floor, do the dishes, take out the trash, sort the laundry, go to the market, start the dinner...
© 1993 MARGIE CHERRY

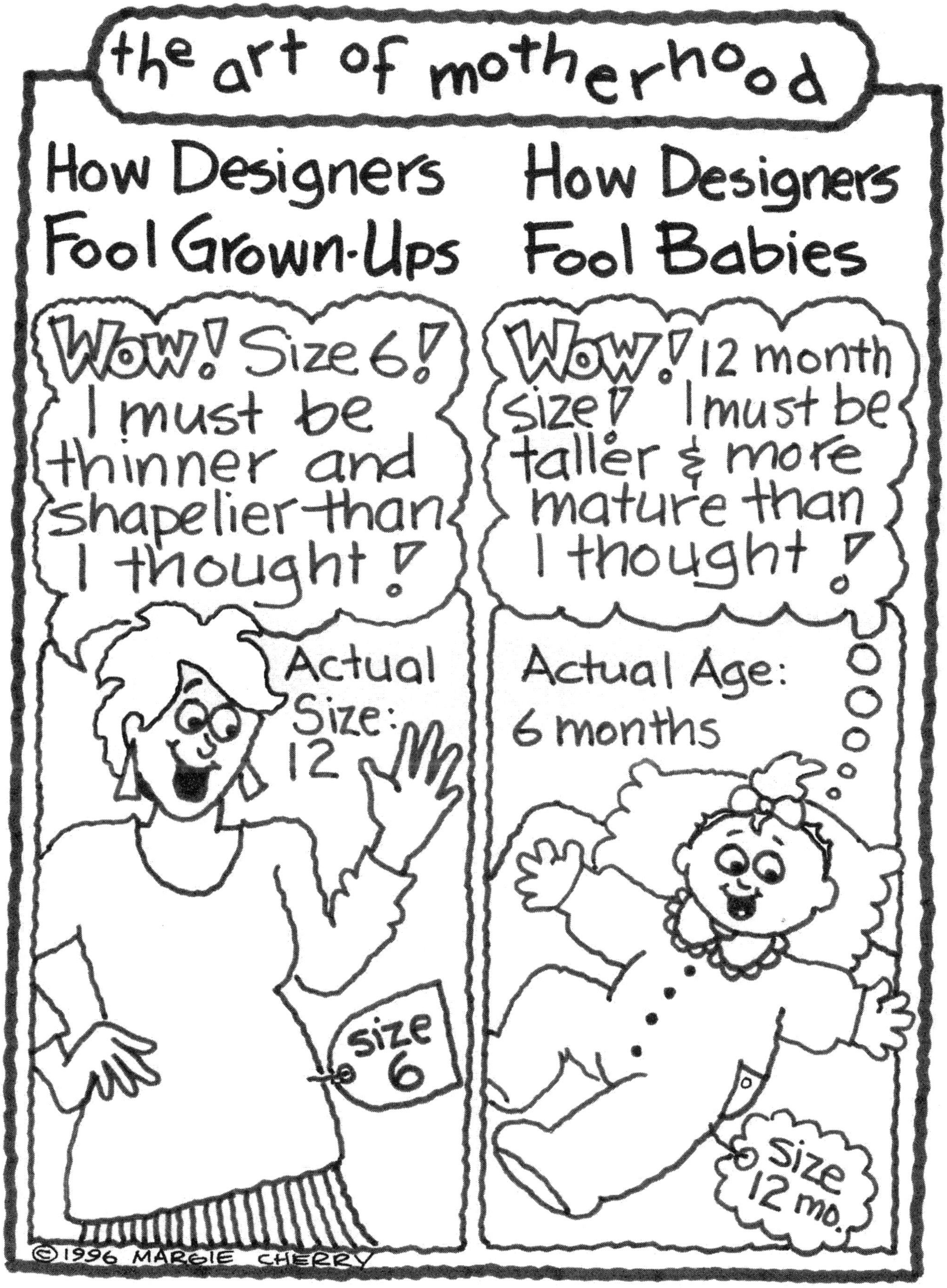
the art of motherhood
How Designers Fool Grown-Ups
How Designers Fool Babies
Wow! Size 6! I must be thinner and shapelier than I thought!
Actual Size: 12
size 6
Wow! 12 month size! I must be taller & more mature than I thought!
Actual Age: 6 months
size 12 mo.
©1996 MARGIE CHERRY

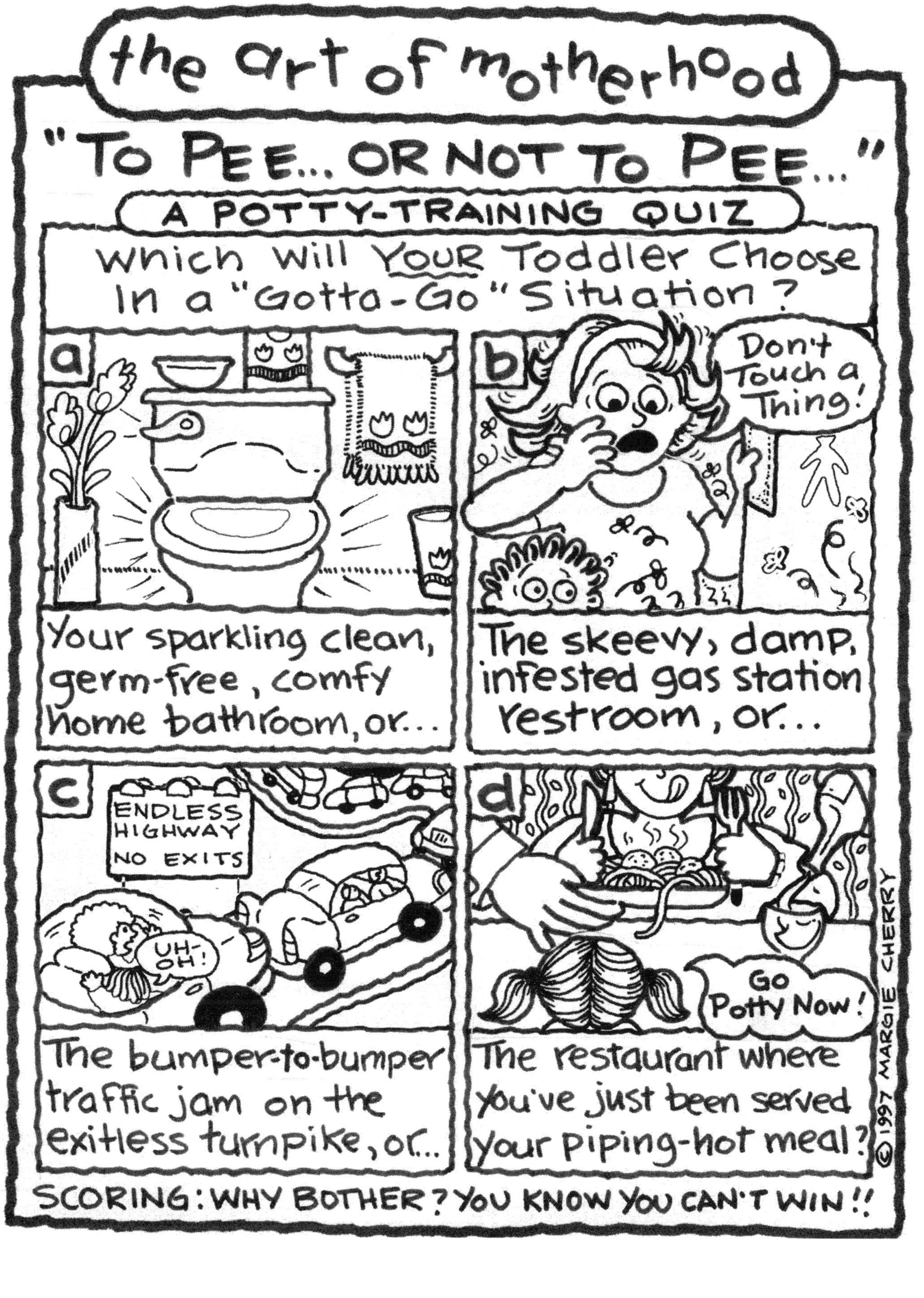
the art of motherhood
"TO PEE... OR NOT TO PEE..."
A POTTY-TRAINING QUIZ
Which Will YOUR Toddler Choose In a "Gotta-Go" Situation?
a
Your sparkling clean, germ-free, comfy home bathroom, or...
b
Don't Touch a Thing!
The skeevy, damp, infested gas station restroom, or...
c
ENDLESS HIGHWAY NO EXITS
UH-OH!
The bumper-to-bumper traffic jam on the exitless turnpike, or...
d
Go Potty Now!
The restaurant where you've just been served your piping-hot meal?
© 1997 MARGIE CHERRY
SCORING: WHY BOTHER? YOU KNOW YOU CAN'T WIN!!

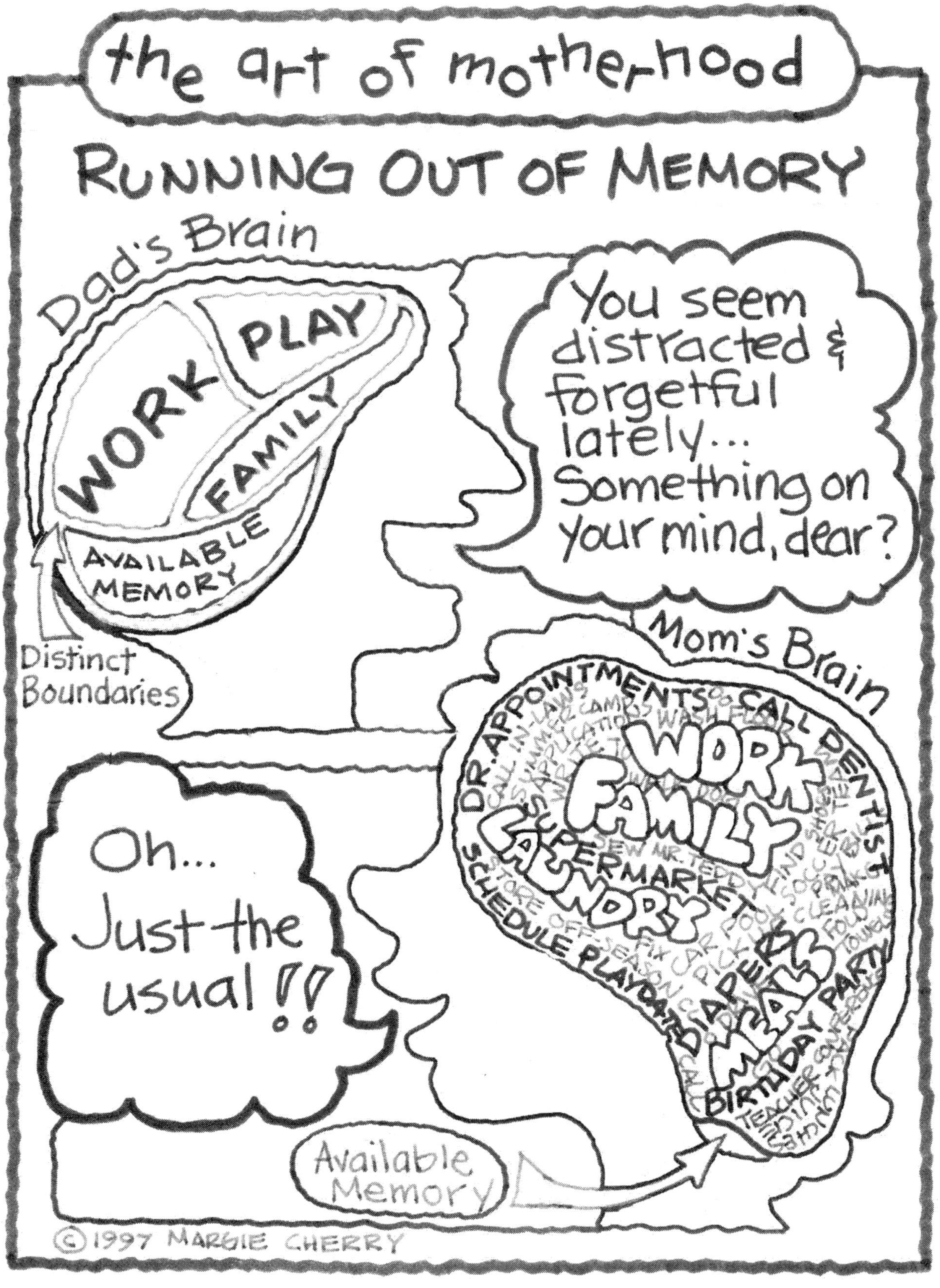
the art of motherhood
RUNNING OUT OF MEMORY
Dad's Brain
PLAY
WORK
FAMILY
AVAILABLE MEMORY
Distinct Boundaries
You seem distracted & forgetful lately... Something on your mind, dear?
Mom's Brain
DR. APPOINTMENTS
CALL DENTIST
WASH FLOOR
WORK
FAMILY
LAUNDRY
SUPERMARKET
SEW MR. TEDDY
SCHEDULE PLAYDATE
DIAPERS
MEALS
BIRTHDAY PARTY
Oh... Just the usual!!
Available Memory
© 1997 MARGIE CHERRY

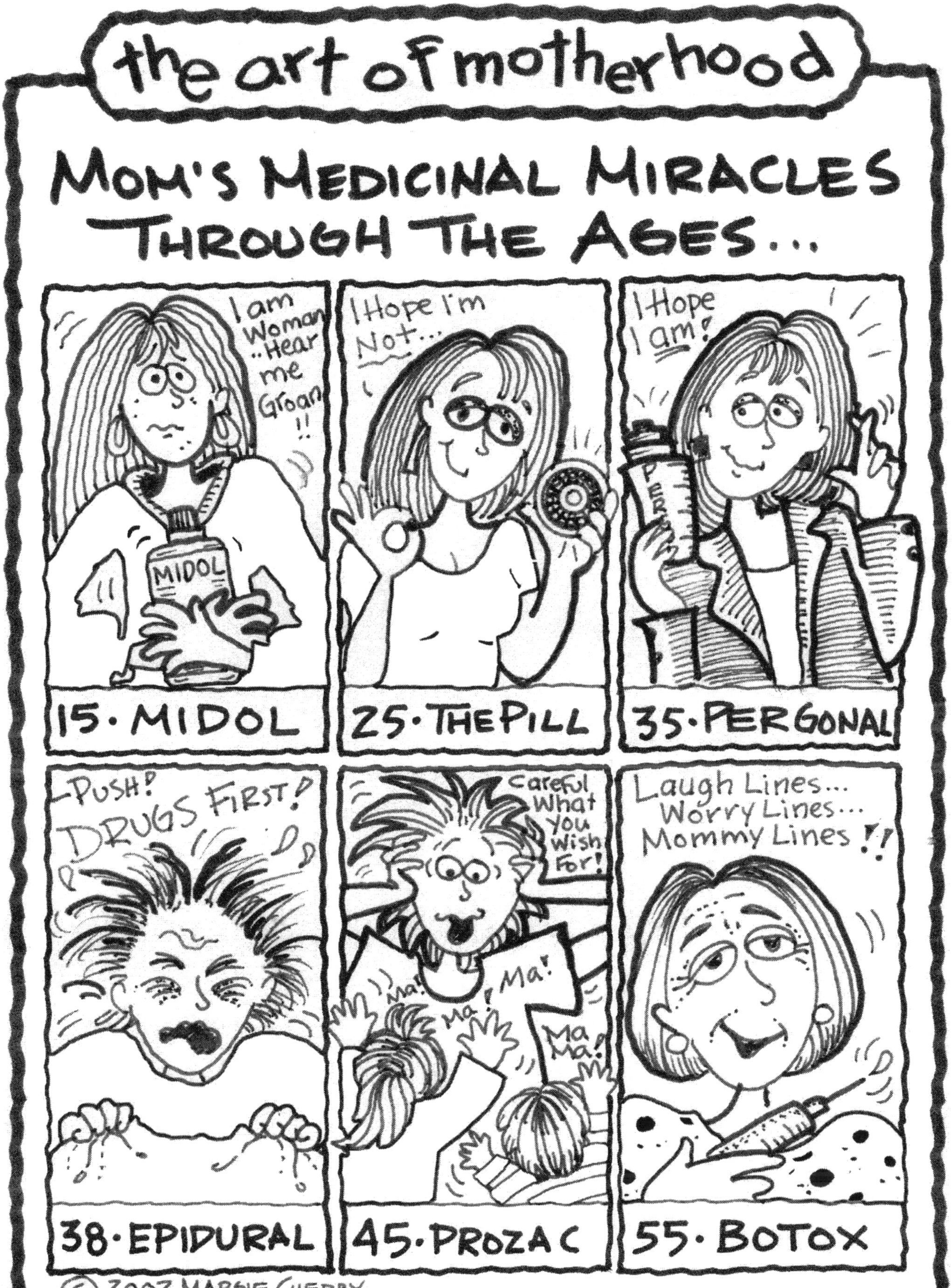
the art of motherhood
MOM'S MEDICINAL MIRACLES THROUGH THE AGES...
I am Woman ..Hear me Groan !!
MIDOL
15 • MIDOL
I Hope I'm Not...
25 • THE PILL
I Hope I am!
35 • PERGONAL
PUSH! DRUGS FIRST!
38 • EPIDURAL
Careful What You Wish For!
Ma! Ma! Ma! Ma Ma!
45 • PROZAC
Laugh Lines... Worry Lines... Mommy Lines !!
55 • BOTOX
© 2002 MARGIE CHERRY

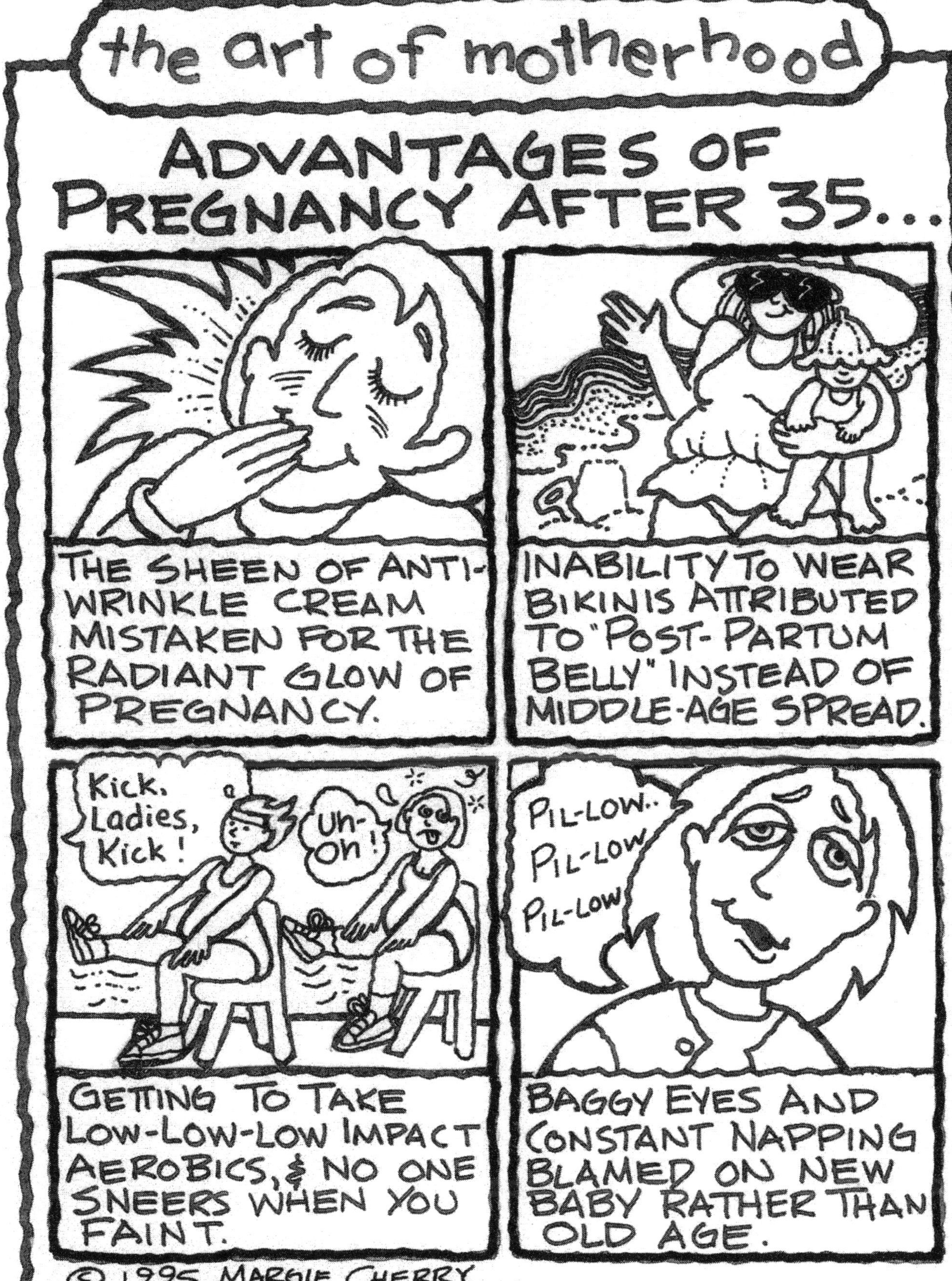
the art of motherhood
ADVANTAGES OF PREGNANCY AFTER 35...
THE SHEEN OF ANTI-WRINKLE CREAM MISTAKEN FOR THE RADIANT GLOW OF PREGNANCY.
INABILITY TO WEAR BIKINIS ATTRIBUTED TO "POST-PARTUM BELLY" INSTEAD OF MIDDLE-AGE SPREAD.
Kick, Ladies, Kick!
Uh-Oh!
GETTING TO TAKE LOW-LOW-LOW IMPACT AEROBICS, & NO ONE SNEERS WHEN YOU FAINT.
PIL-LOW..
PIL-LOW
PIL-LOW
BAGGY EYES AND CONSTANT NAPPING BLAMED ON NEW BABY RATHER THAN OLD AGE.
© 1995 MARGIE CHERRY

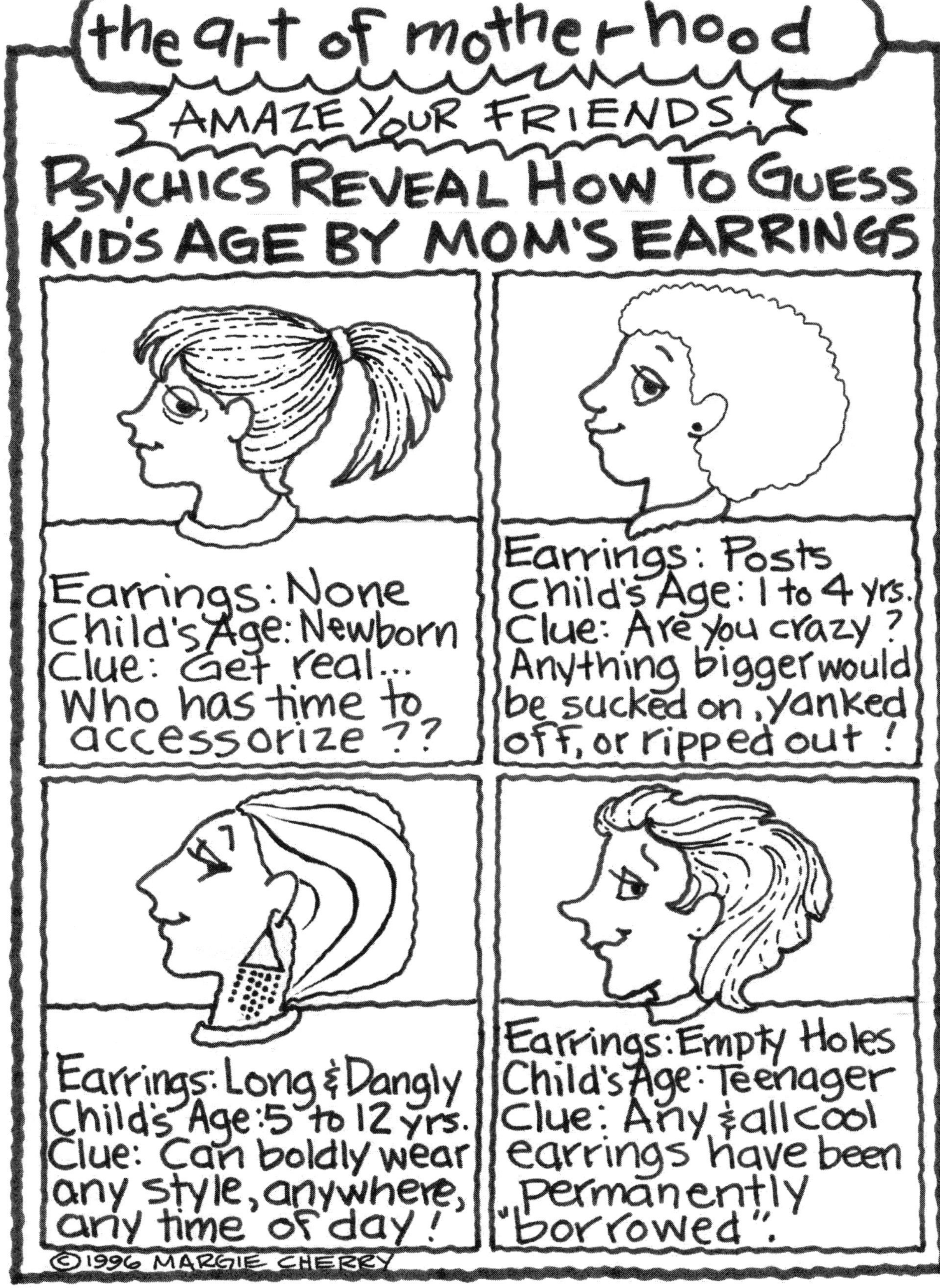
the art of motherhood
AMAZE YOUR FRIENDS!
PSYCHICS REVEAL HOW TO GUESS KID'S AGE BY MOM'S EARRINGS
Earrings: None
Child's Age: Newborn
Clue: Get real... Who has time to accessorize ??
Earrings: Posts
Child's Age: 1 to 4 yrs.
Clue: Are you crazy? Anything bigger would be sucked on, yanked off, or ripped out!
Earrings: Long & Dangly
Child's Age: 5 to 12 yrs.
Clue: Can boldly wear any style, anywhere, any time of day!
Earrings: Empty Holes
Child's Age: Teenager
Clue: Any & all cool earrings have been permanently "borrowed".
©1996 MARGIE CHERRY

# the art of motherhood

## Housekeeping Tips For Busy Moms

### WHY BUY THIS:

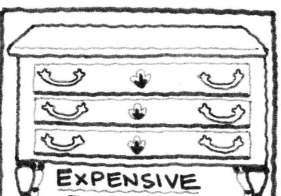

**EXPENSIVE DRESSERS** REQUIRE YOU TO FOLD OR EVEN IRON YOUR CLOTHES BEFORE STORING. BORING!

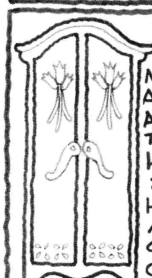

**FANCY ARMOIRES** MAY LEAD TO AN EXPENSIVE ADDICTION TO SATIN HANGERS & SACHETS. HIDES AWAY ALL YOUR COLORFUL CLOTHING.

### WHEN YOU CAN USE THIS:

**LAUNDRY BASKETS** PROVIDE CHEAP, NO-SWEAT STORAGE AND TURN EVERY MORNING INTO AN EXCITING TREASURE HUNT !!

**UNUSED EXERCISE EQUIPMENT** EASILY DISPLAYS YOUR FAVORITE OUTFITS & KEEPS THEM WITHIN REACH !!

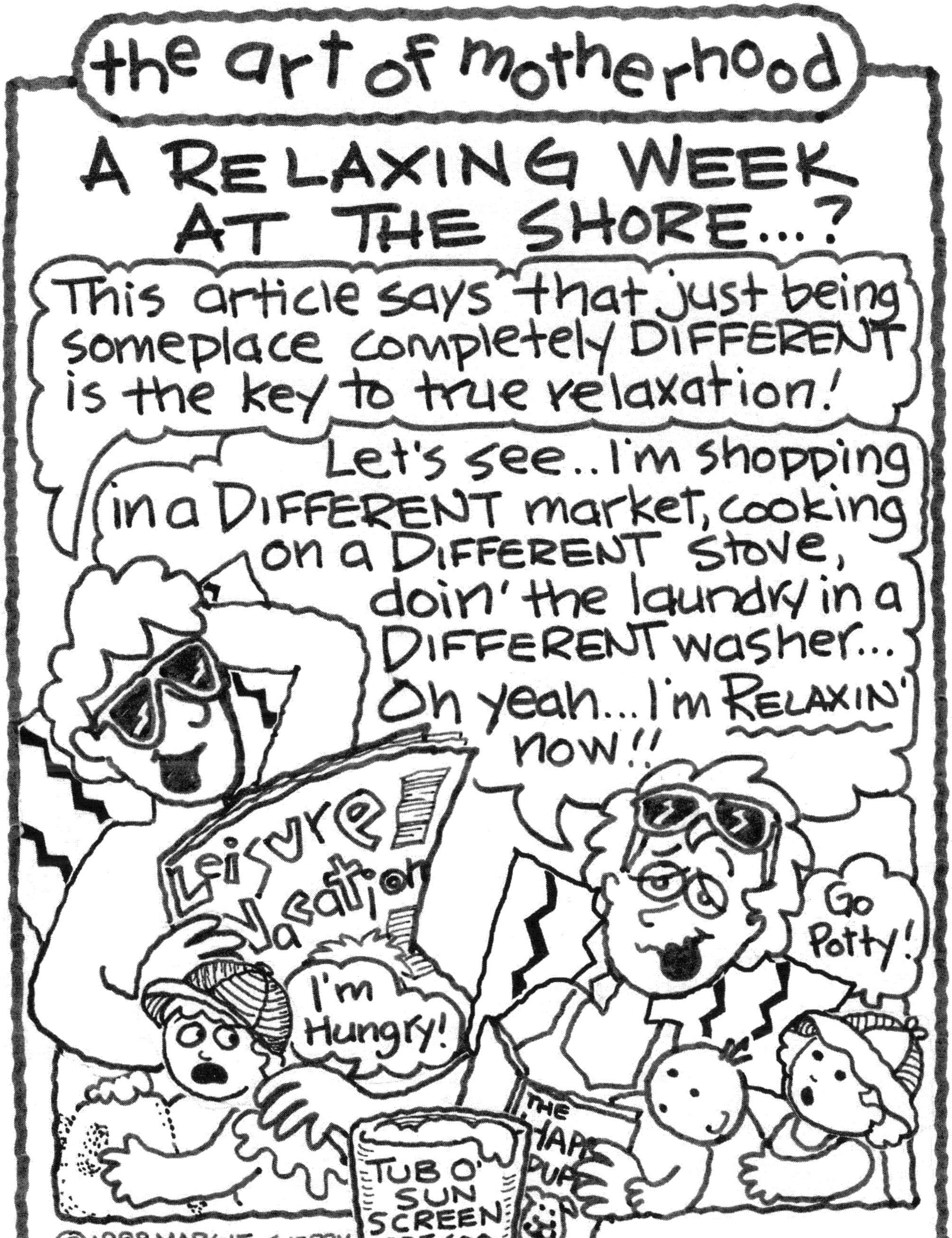
the art of motherhood
A RELAXING WEEK AT THE SHORE...?
This article says that just being someplace completely DIFFERENT is the key to true relaxation!
Let's see... I'm shopping in a DIFFERENT market, cooking on a DIFFERENT stove, doin' the laundry in a DIFFERENT washer... Oh yeah... I'm RELAXIN' now!!
Leisure Vacation
I'm Hungry!
Go Potty!
TUB O' SUN SCREEN SPF 600
©1999 MARGIE CHERRY

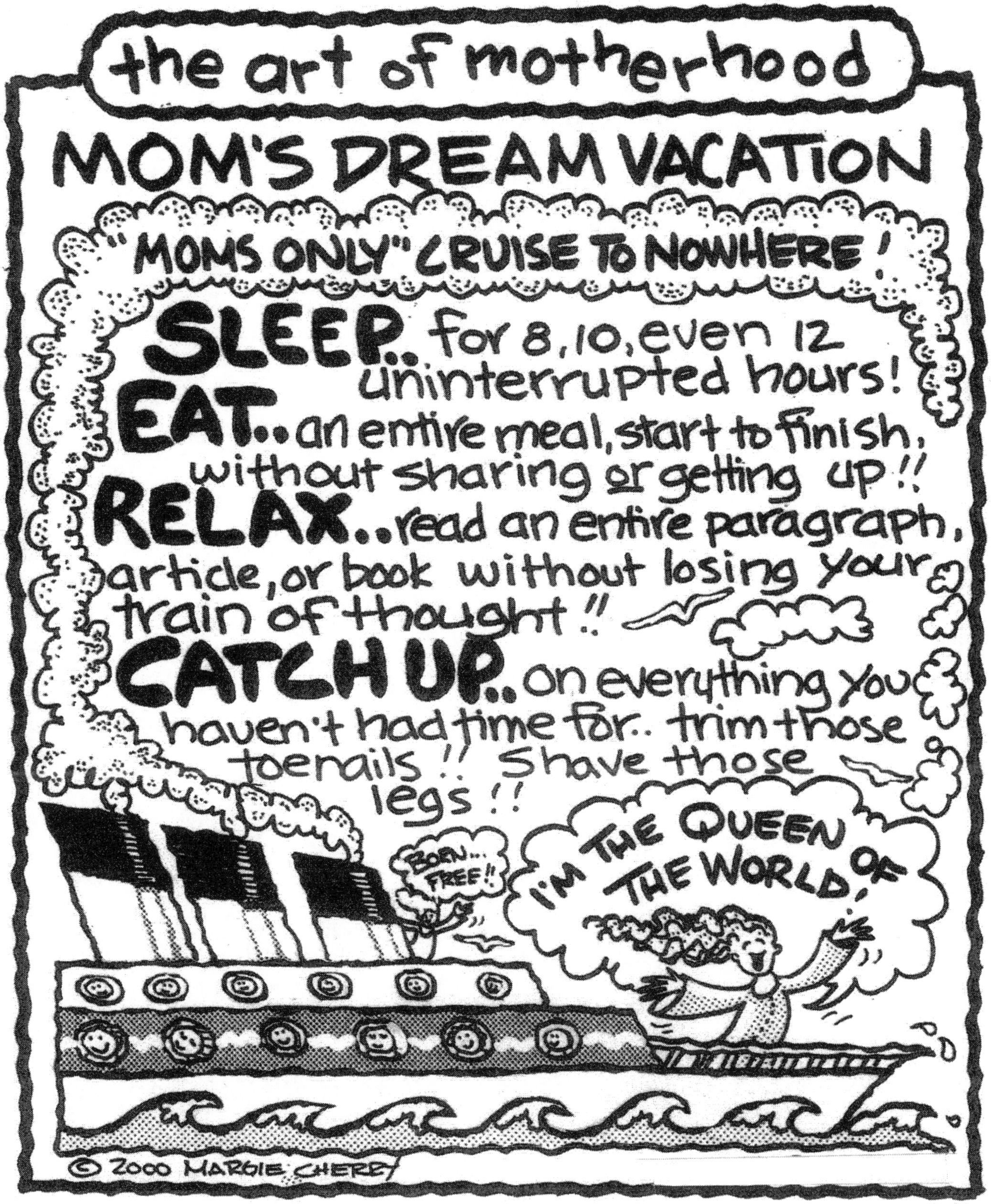

the art of motherhood
MOM'S DREAM VACATION
"MOMS ONLY" CRUISE TO NOWHERE!
SLEEP.. for 8, 10, even 12 uninterrupted hours!
EAT.. an entire meal, start to finish, without sharing or getting up!!
RELAX.. read an entire paragraph, article, or book without losing your train of thought!!
CATCH UP.. on everything you haven't had time for.. trim those toenails!! Shave those legs!!
BORN... FREE!!
I'M THE QUEEN OF THE WORLD!
© 2000 MARGIE CHERRY

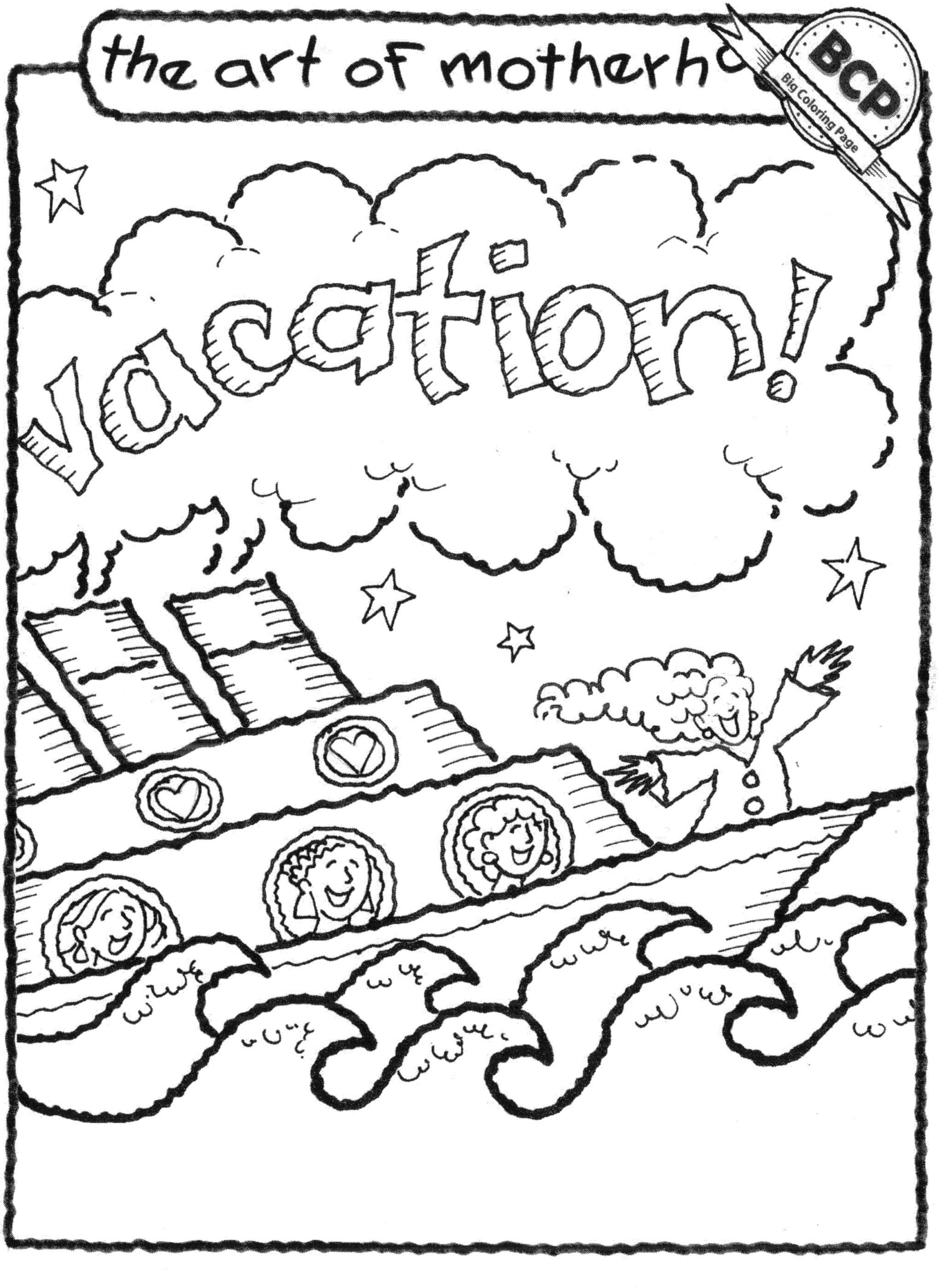
the art of motherho
BCP
Big Coloring Page
vacation!

CIY
Cartoon-It-Yourself

YOUR MOM-CATION

# Mom-tainment

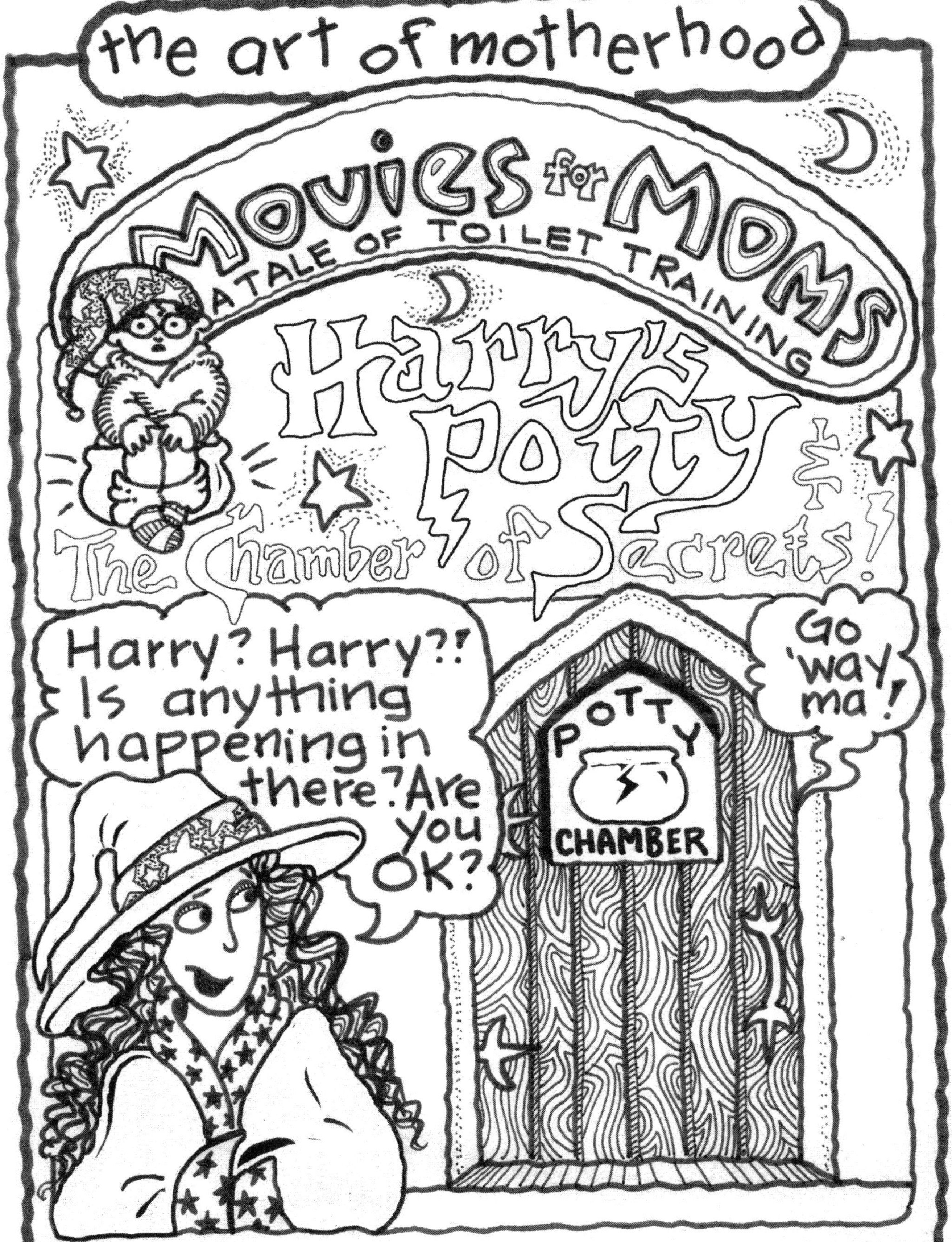
the art of motherhood
Movies for Moms
A TALE OF TOILET TRAINING
Harry's Potty & The Chamber of Secrets!
Harry? Harry?! Is anything happening in there? Are you OK?
Go 'way, ma!
POTTY
CHAMBER

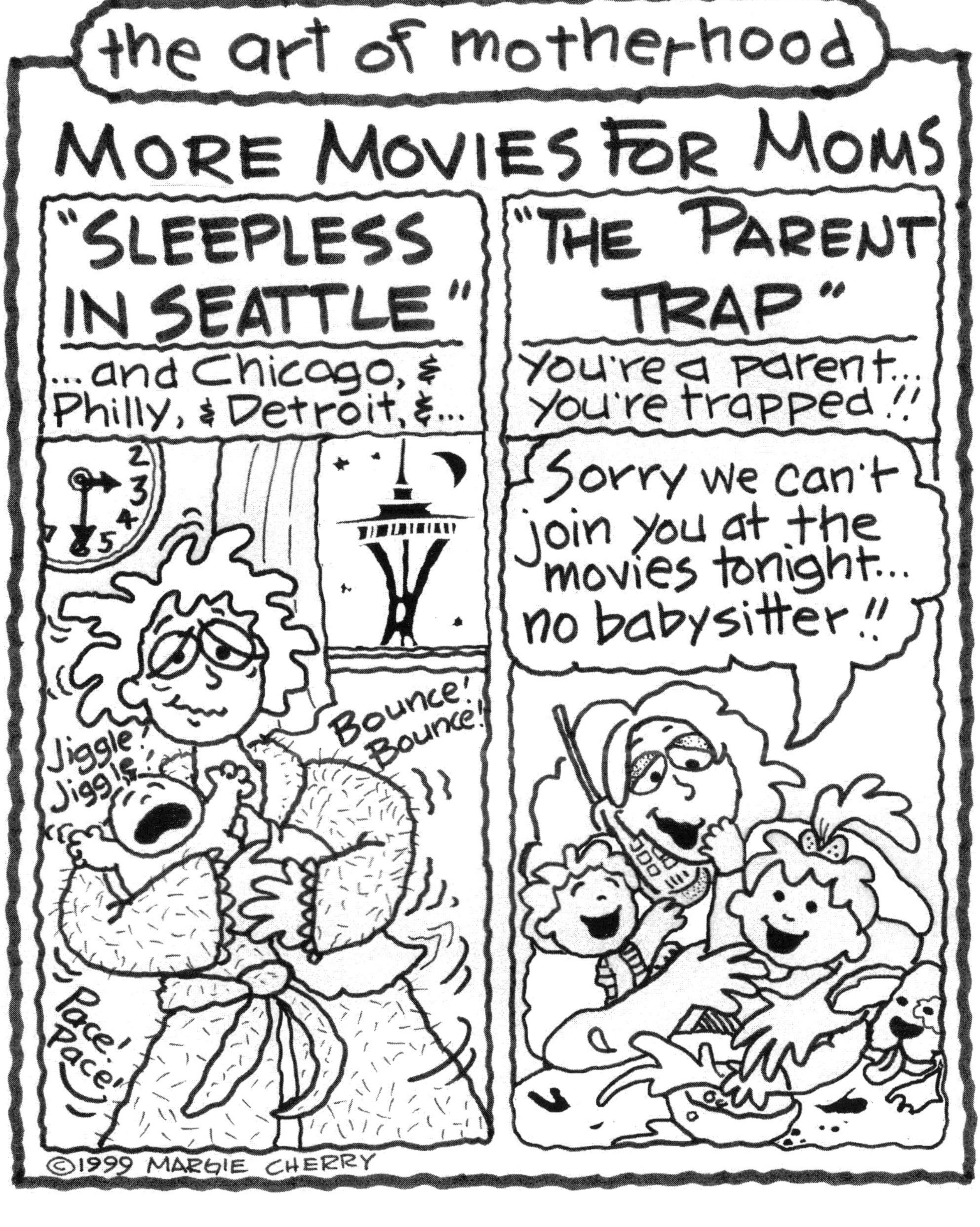
the art of motherhood
MORE MOVIES FOR MOMS
"SLEEPLESS IN SEATTLE"
...and Chicago, & Philly, & Detroit, &...
Jiggle! Jiggle!
Bounce! Bounce!
Pace! Pace!
"THE PARENT TRAP"
You're a parent... You're trapped!!
Sorry we can't join you at the movies tonight... no babysitter!!
©1999 MARGIE CHERRY

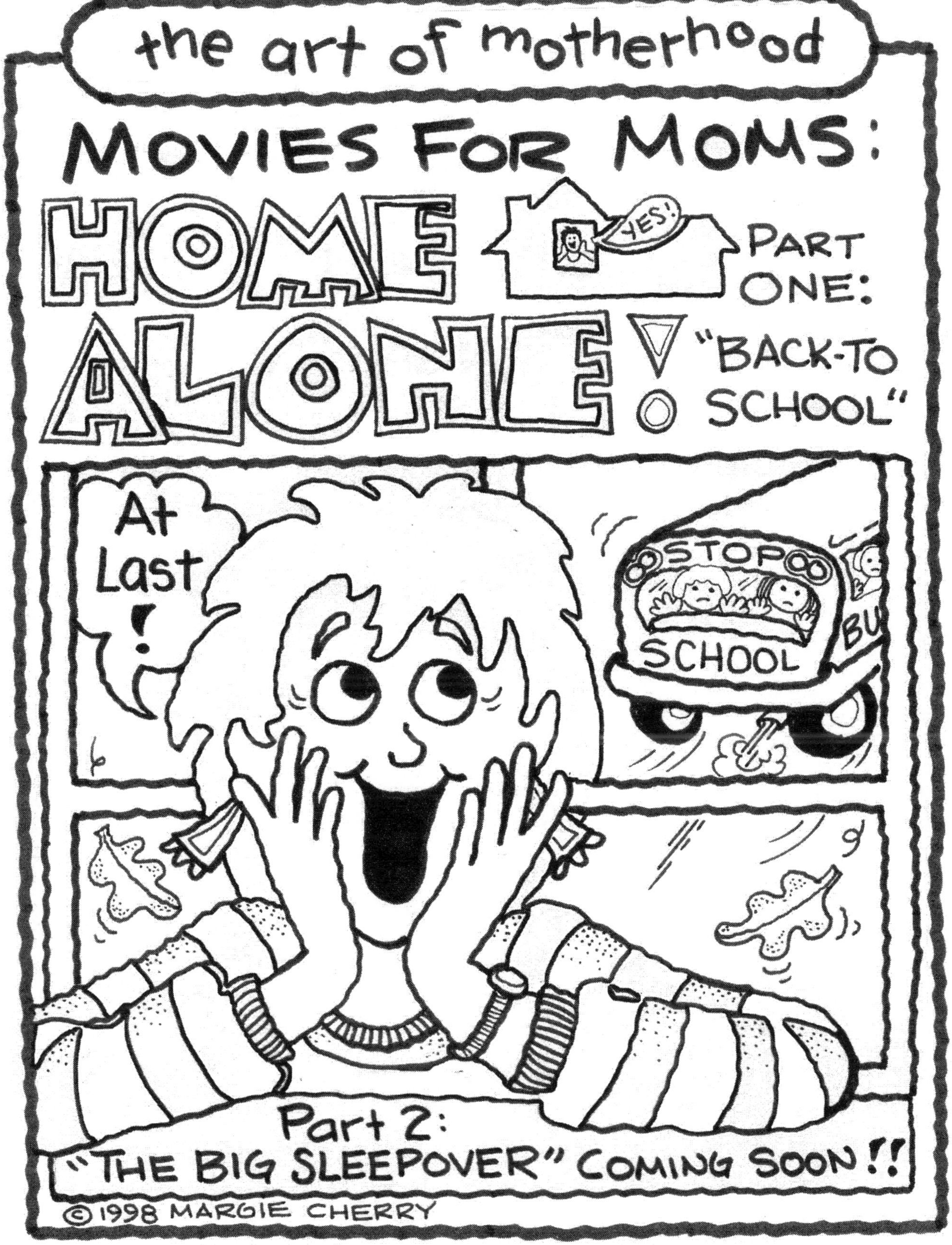
the art of motherhood
MOVIES FOR MOMS:
HOME ALONE!
YES!
PART ONE: "BACK-TO SCHOOL"
At Last!
STOP
SCHOOL
BU
Part 2: "THE BIG SLEEPOVER" COMING SOON!!
© 1998 MARGIE CHERRY

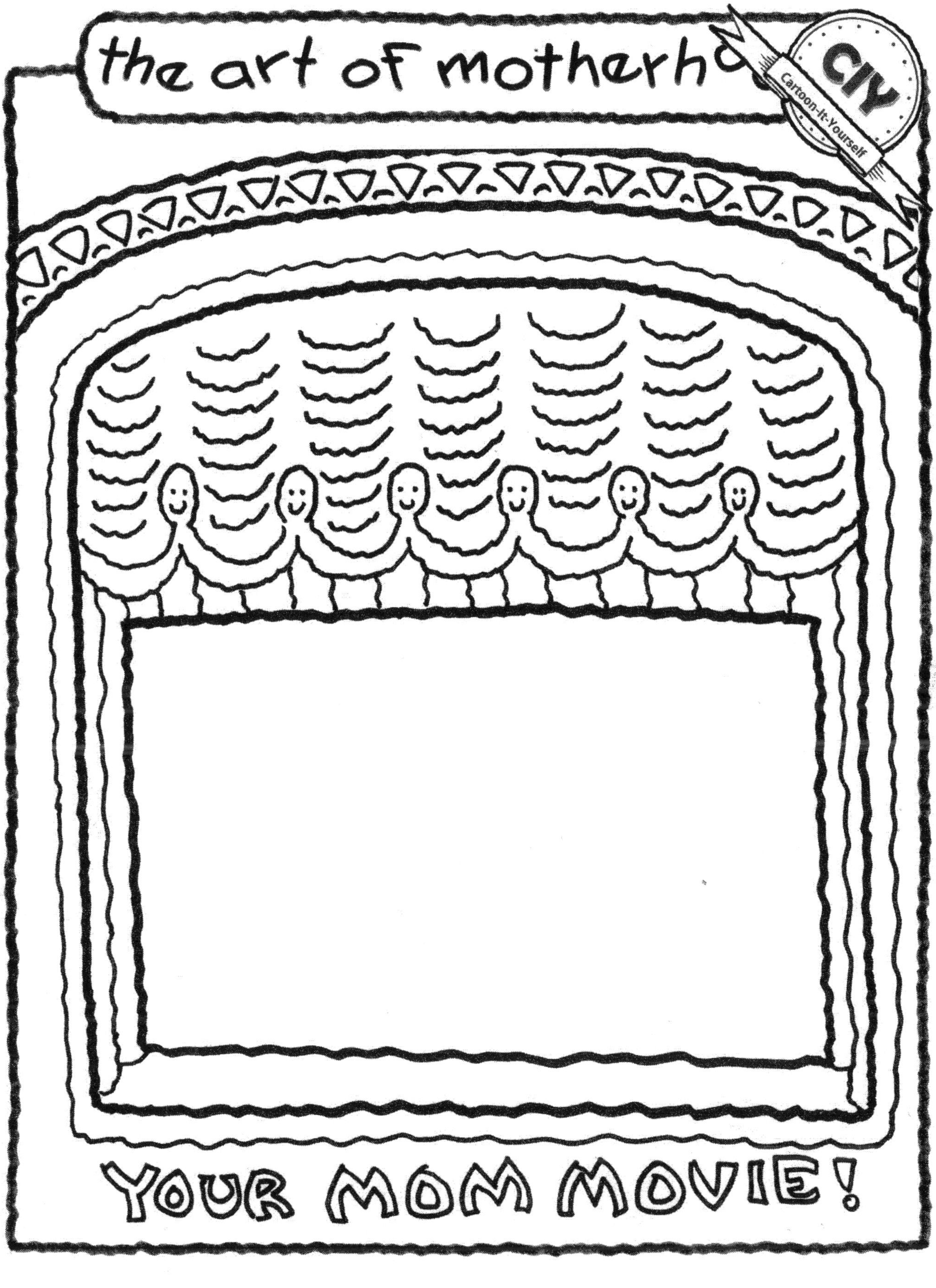
the art of motherho
CIY
Cartoon-It-Yourself
YOUR MOM MOVIE!

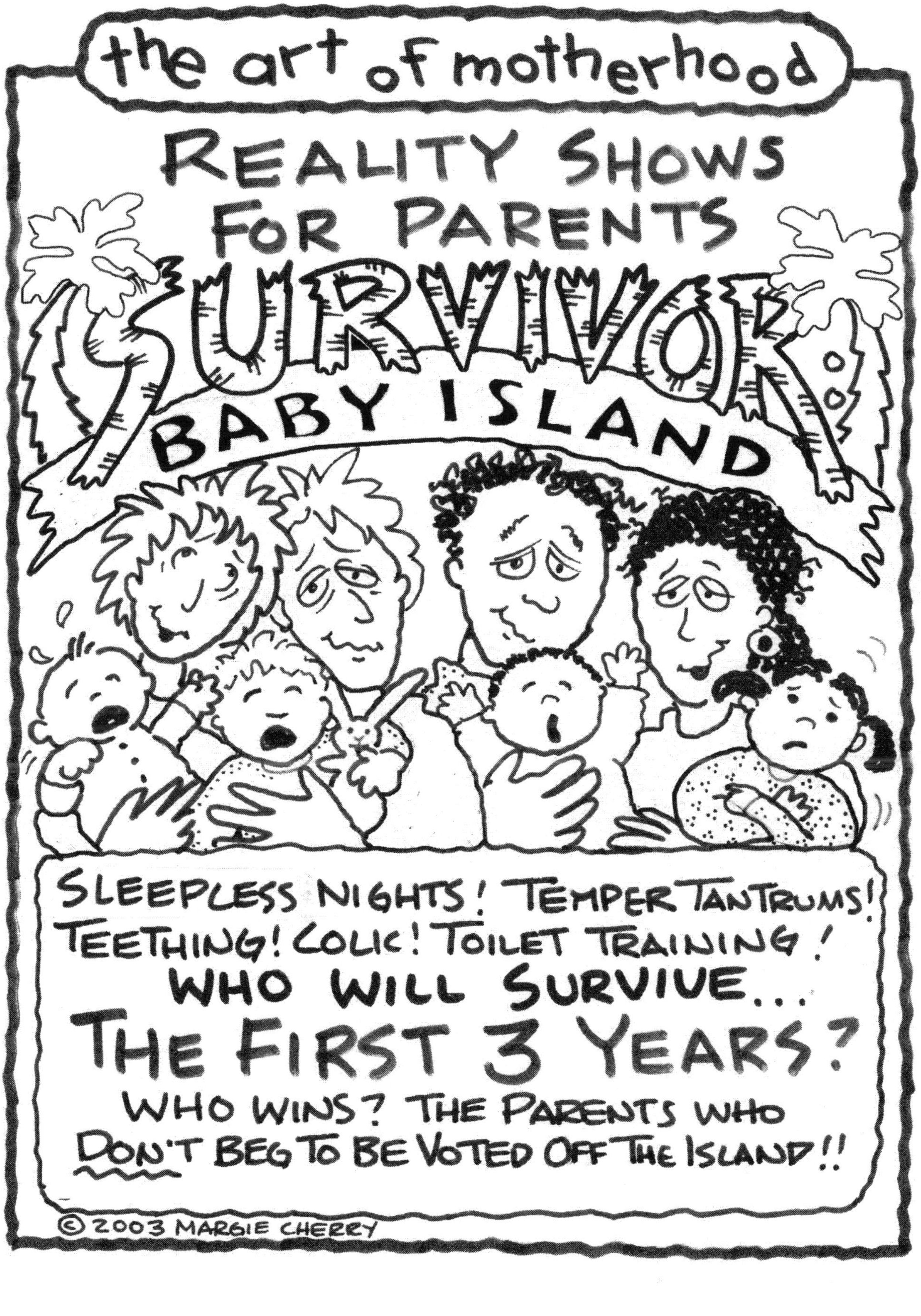
the art of motherhood
REALITY SHOWS FOR PARENTS
SURVIVOR: BABY ISLAND
SLEEPLESS NIGHTS! TEMPER TANTRUMS!
TEETHING! COLIC! TOILET TRAINING!
WHO WILL SURVIVE...
THE FIRST 3 YEARS?
WHO WINS? THE PARENTS WHO
DON'T BEG TO BE VOTED OFF THE ISLAND!!
© 2003 MARGIE CHERRY

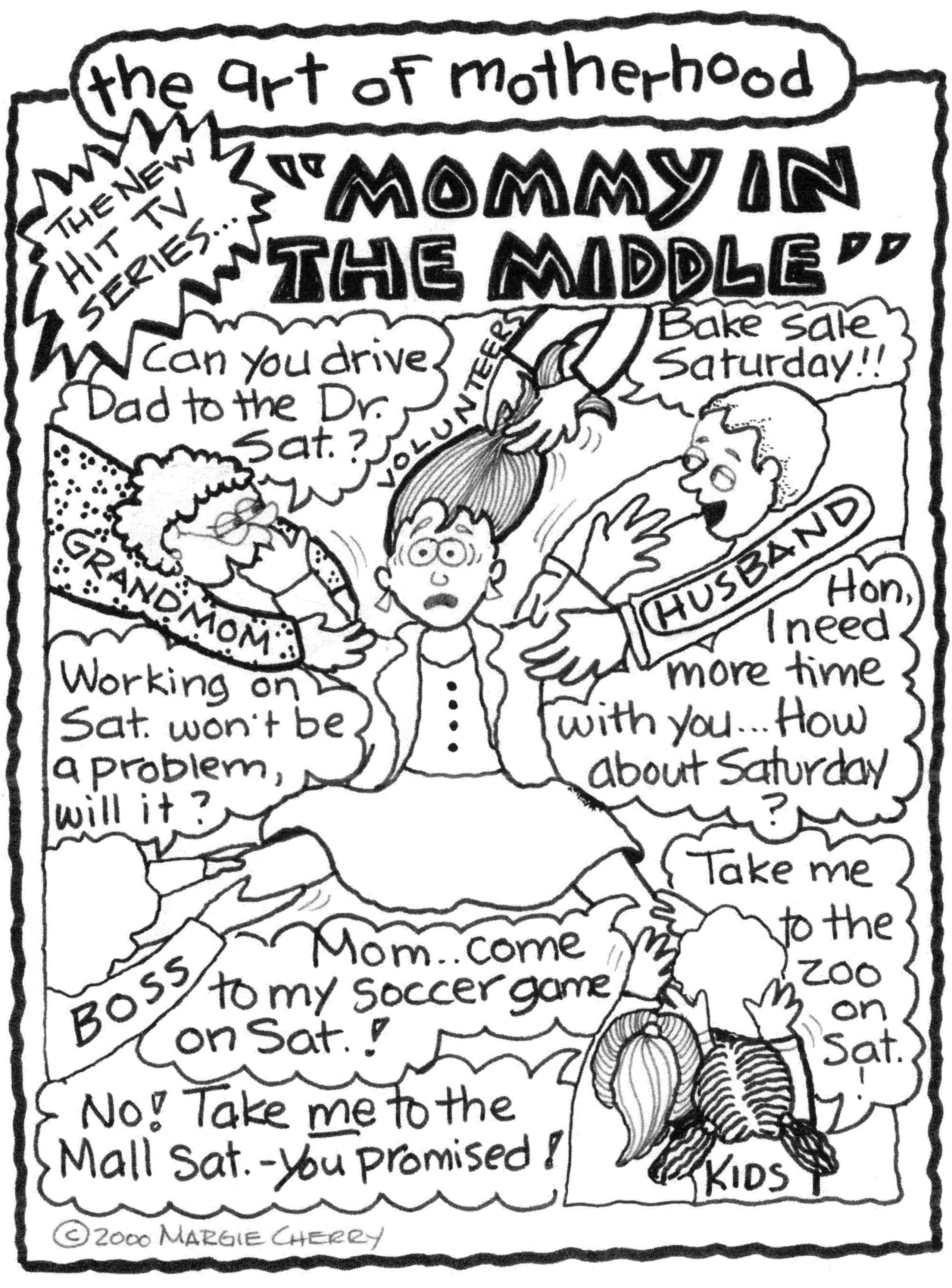
the art of motherhood
THE NEW HIT TV SERIES...
"MOMMY IN THE MIDDLE"
Can you drive Dad to the Dr. Sat.?
VOLUNTEER
Bake sale Saturday!!
GRANDMOM
HUSBAND
Hon, I need more time with you... How about Saturday?
Working on Sat. won't be a problem, will it?
BOSS
Mom..come to my soccer game on Sat.!
Take me to the zoo on Sat.!
No! Take me to the Mall Sat.-You promised!
KIDS
©2000 MARGIE CHERRY

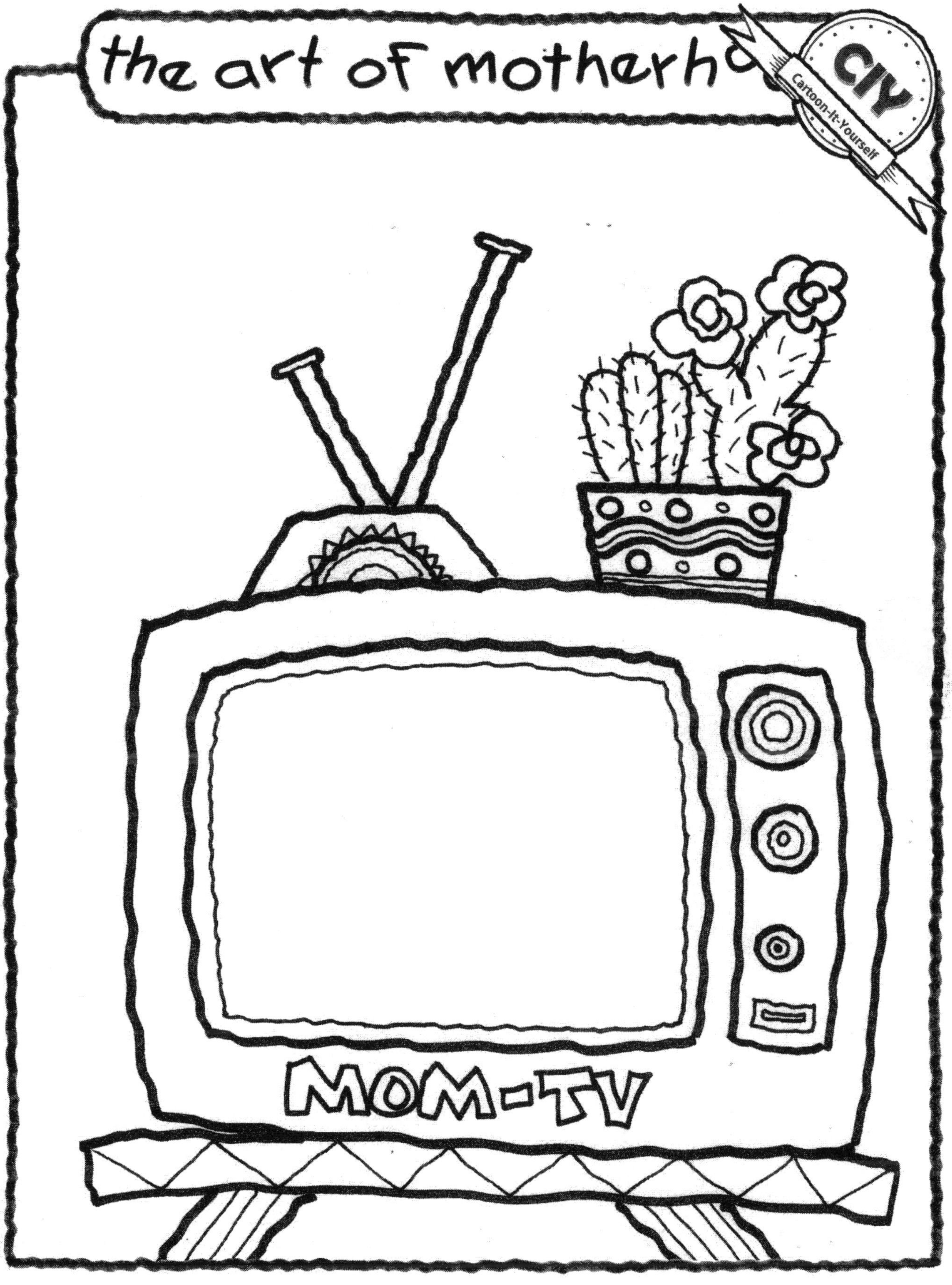
the art of motherho
CIY
Cartoon-It-Yourself
MOM-TV

# Mom-ventions

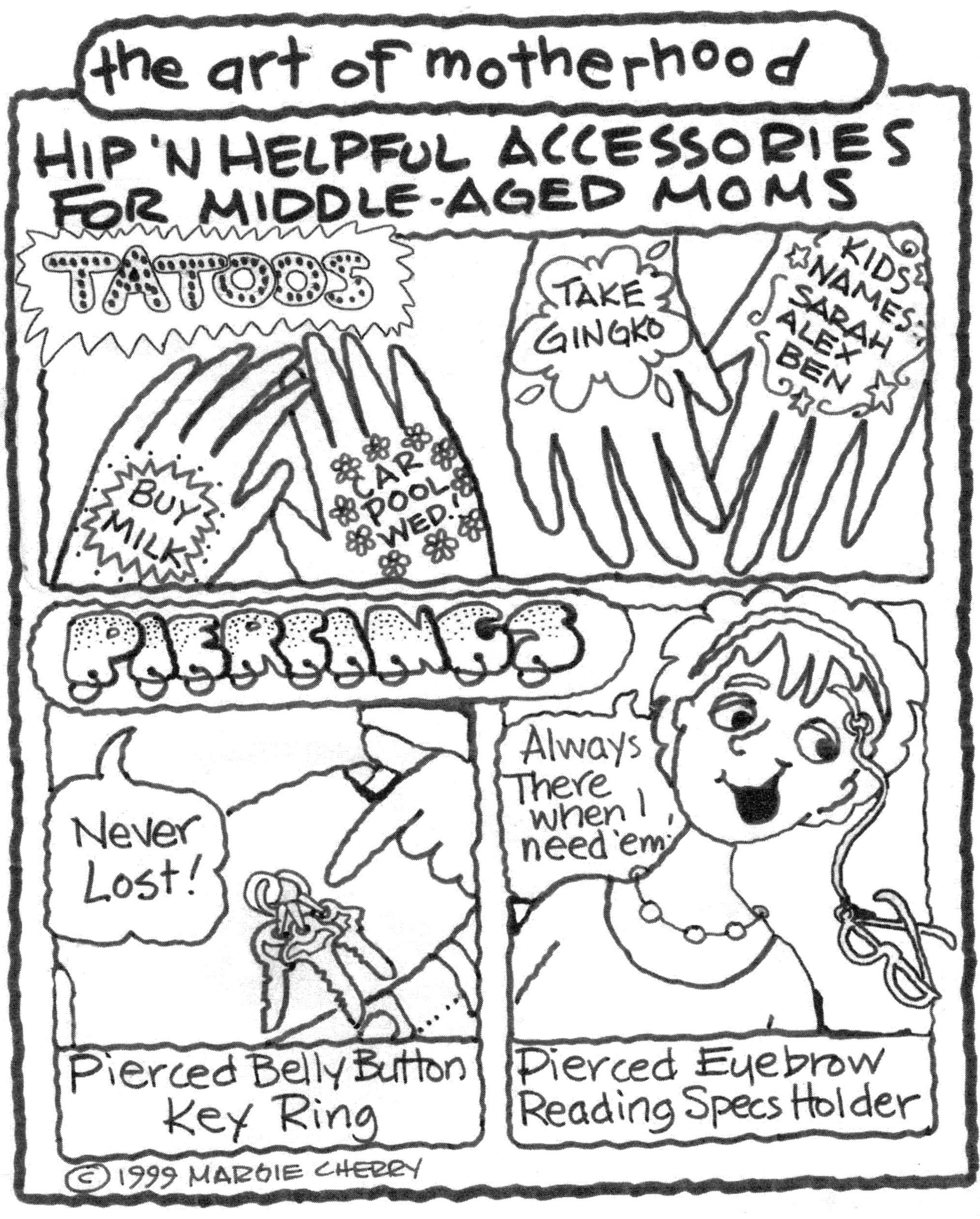
the art of motherhood
HIP 'N HELPFUL ACCESSORIES FOR MIDDLE-AGED MOMS
TATOOS
BUY MILK
CAR POOL WED!
TAKE GINGKO
KIDS NAMES: SARAH ALEX BEN
PIERCINGS
Never Lost!
Pierced Belly Button Key Ring
Always There when I need 'em!
Pierced Eyebrow Reading Specs Holder
© 1999 MARGIE CHERRY

# The Only Tattoos We'll Let Our Children Get

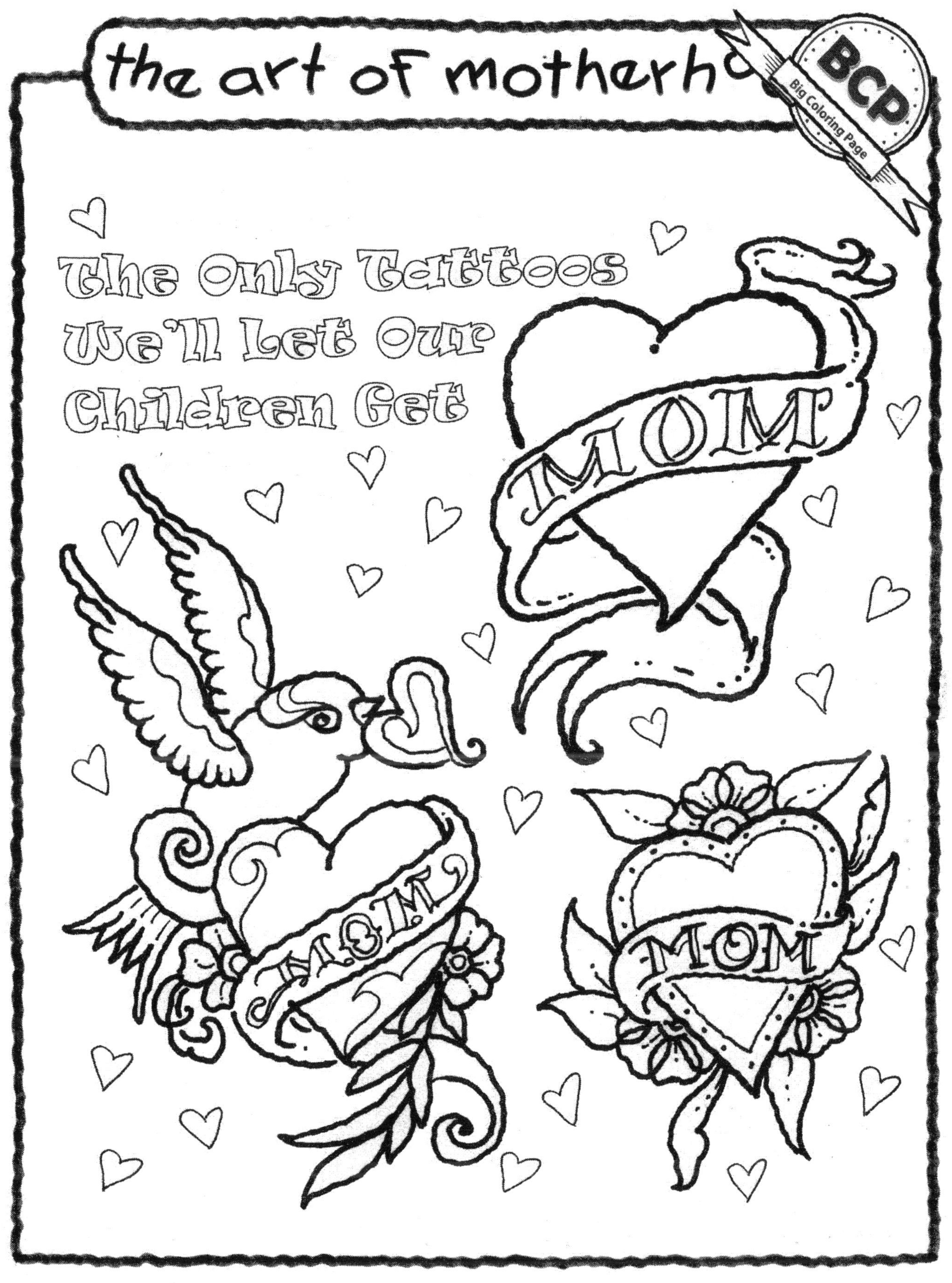
MOM
MOM
MOM

CIY
Cartoon-It-Yourself

Design Your Own
MOM-TAT

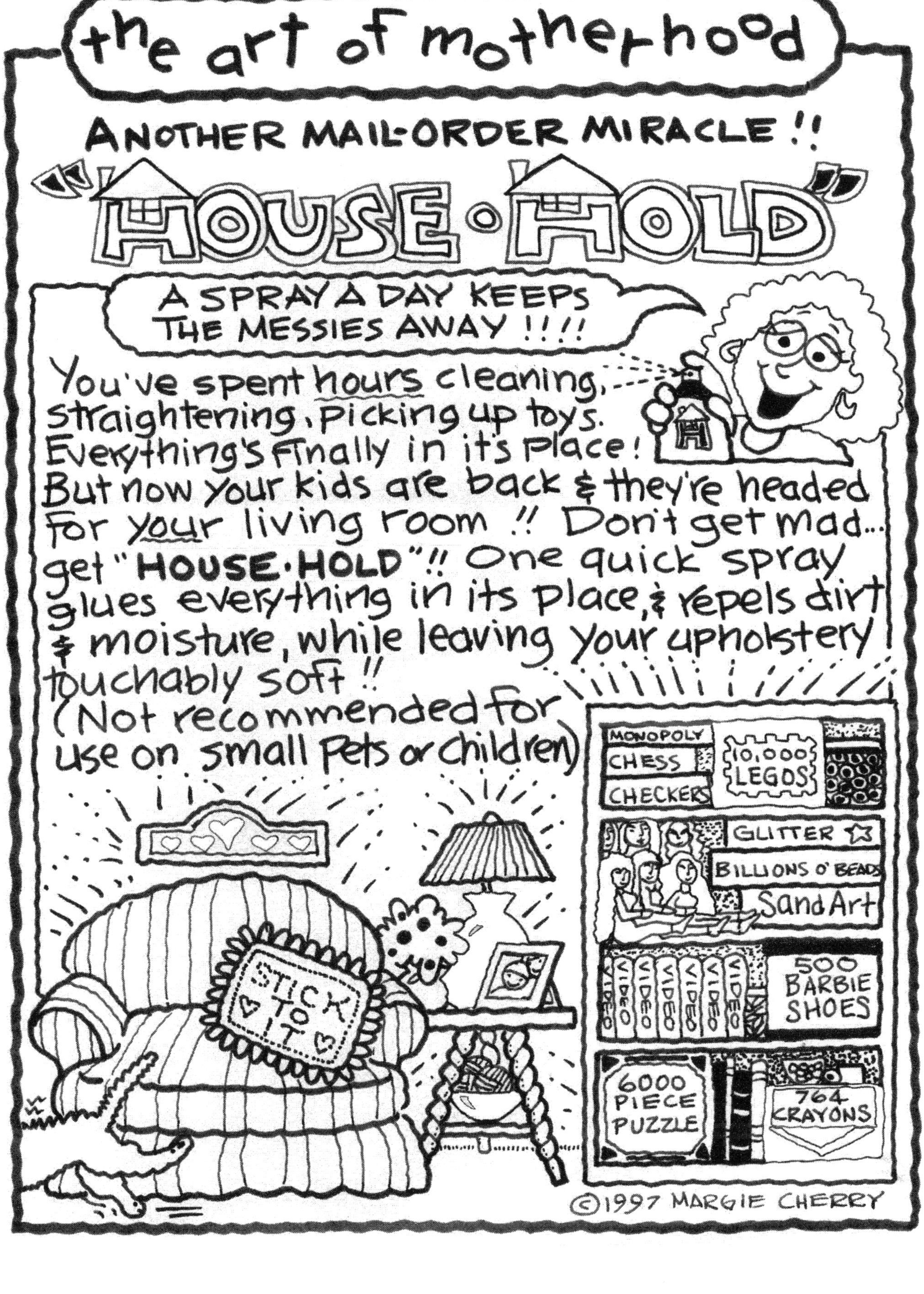
the art of motherhood
ANOTHER MAIL-ORDER MIRACLE !!
"HOUSE·HOLD"
A SPRAY A DAY KEEPS THE MESSIES AWAY !!!!
You've spent hours cleaning, straightening, picking up toys. Everything's finally in it's place! But now your kids are back & they're headed for your living room !! Don't get mad... get "HOUSE·HOLD"!! One quick spray glues everything in its place, & repels dirt & moisture, while leaving your upholstery touchably soft !!
(Not recommended for use on small pets or children)
MONOPOLY
CHESS
CHECKERS
10,000 LEGOS
GLITTER
BILLIONS O' BEADS
Sand Art
VIDEO
VIDEO
VIDEO
VIDEO
VIDEO
VIDEO
500 BARBIE SHOES
6000 PIECE PUZZLE
764 CRAYONS
STICK TO IT
©1997 MARGIE CHERRY

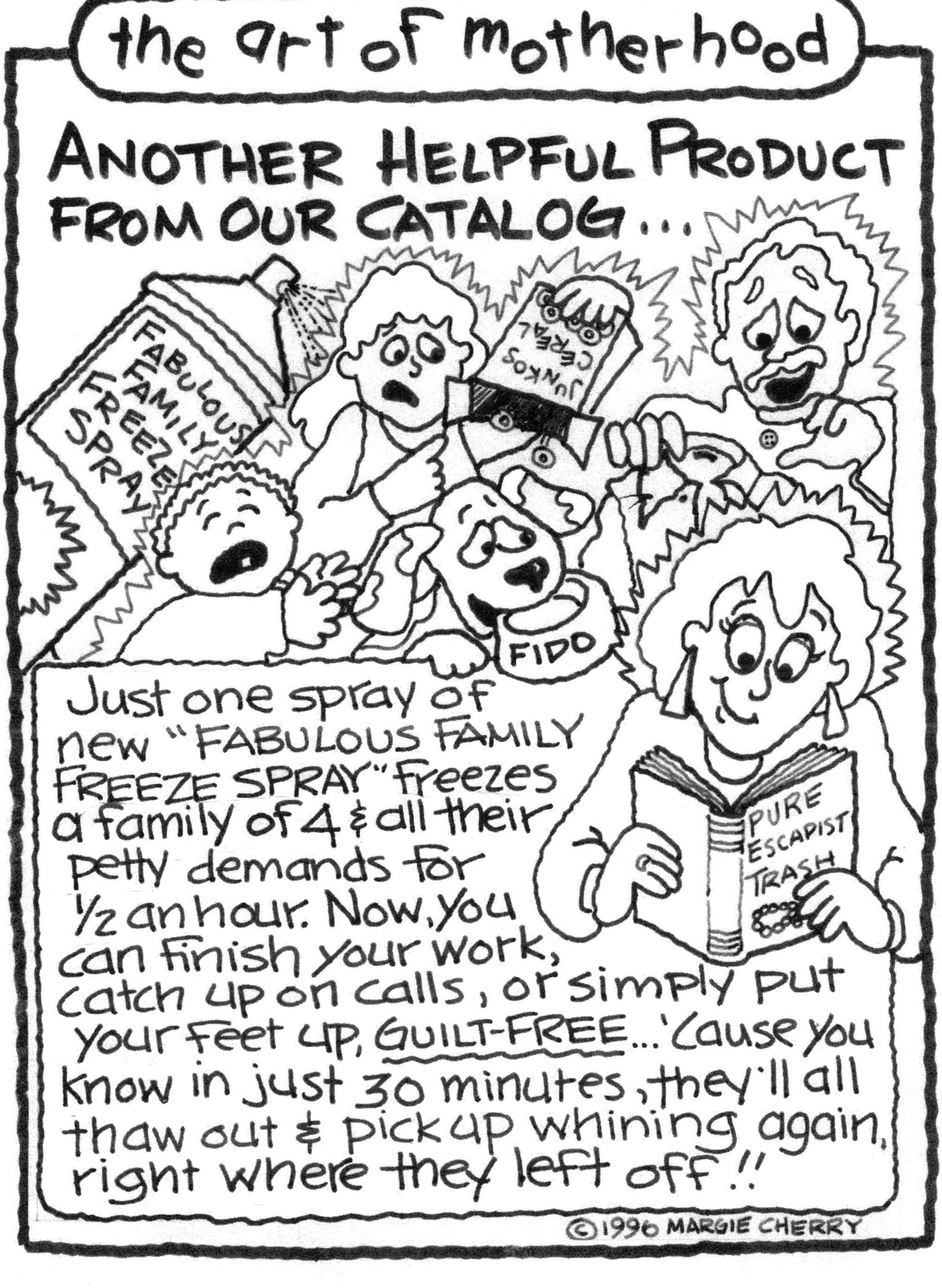
the art of motherhood
ANOTHER HELPFUL PRODUCT FROM OUR CATALOG...
FABULOUS FAMILY FREEZE SPRAY
JUNKOS CEREAL
FIDO
PURE ESCAPIST TRASH
Just one spray of new "FABULOUS FAMILY FREEZE SPRAY" freezes a family of 4 & all their petty demands for 1/2 an hour. Now, you can finish your work, catch up on calls, or simply put your feet up, GUILT-FREE... 'Cause you know in just 30 minutes, they'll all thaw out & pick up whining again, right where they left off!!
©1996 MARGIE CHERRY

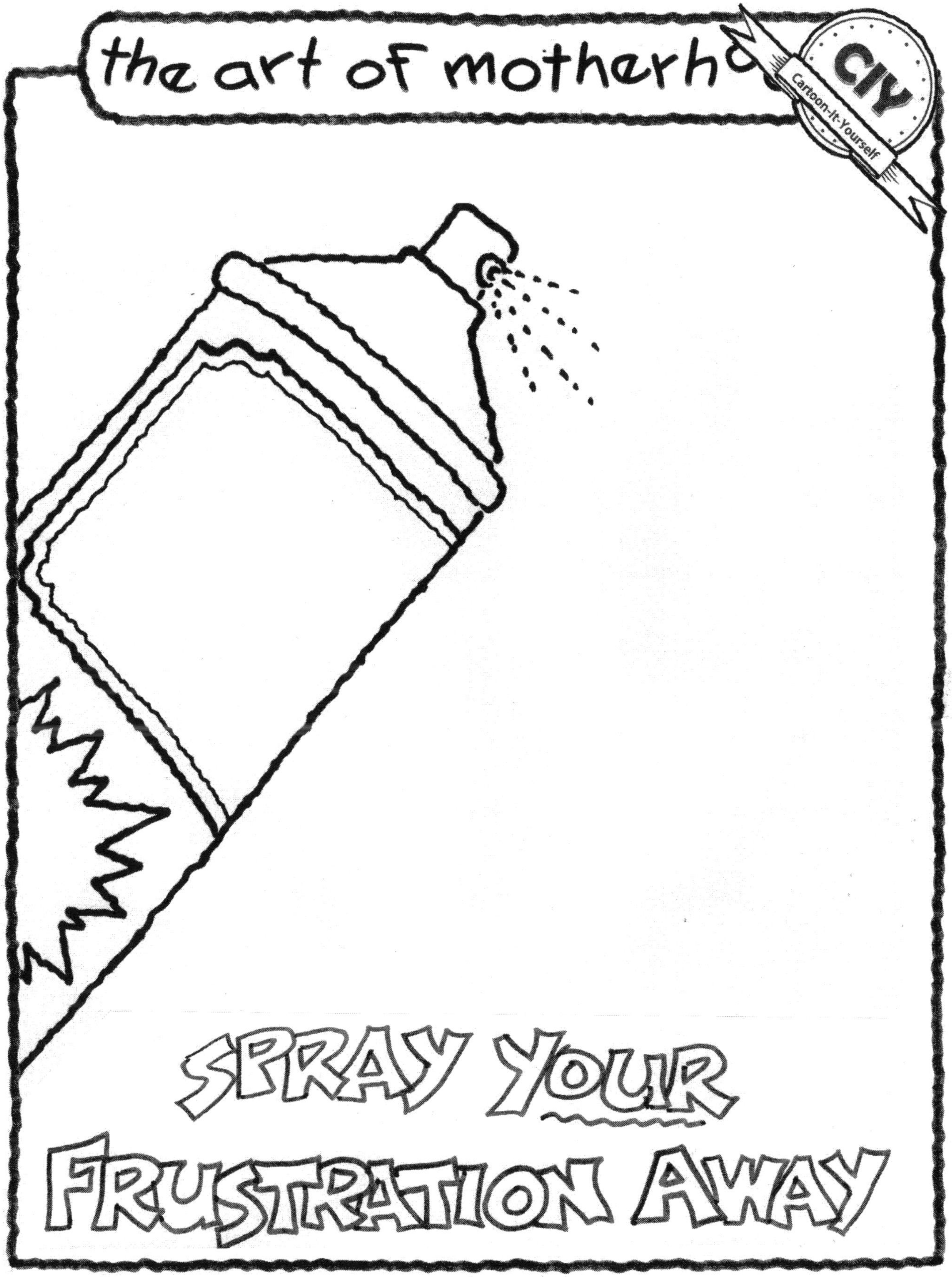
the art of motherho
CIY
Cartoon-It-Yourself
SPRAY YOUR
FRUSTRATION AWAY

## the art of motherhood

# CLONING FOR MOMS

Grow an extra arm with the arrival of each new child !!

**1 CHILD = 1 EXTRA ARM**

Feed the baby and yourself !!

**2 KIDS = 2 EXTRA ARMS**

Diaper the baby and hold your toddler.

**3 KIDS = 3 EXTRA ARMS**

Push the stroller, hold the kids & walk the dog !

"Now if I could just find time for a manicure"

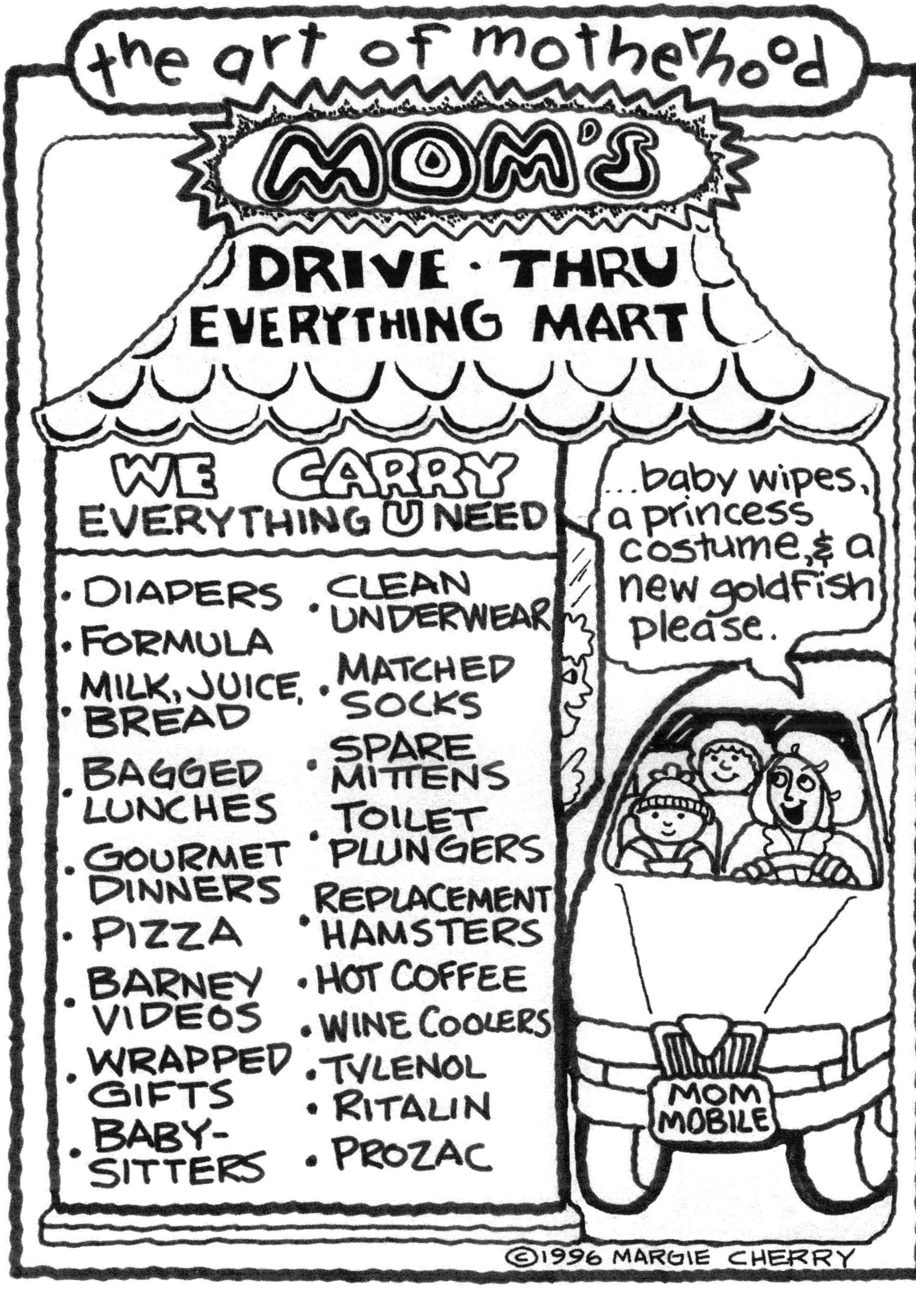
the art of motherhood
MOM'S
DRIVE · THRU
EVERYTHING MART
WE CARRY EVERYTHING U NEED
• DIAPERS
• FORMULA
• MILK, JUICE, BREAD
• BAGGED LUNCHES
• GOURMET DINNERS
• PIZZA
• BARNEY VIDEOS
• WRAPPED GIFTS
• BABY-SITTERS
• CLEAN UNDERWEAR
• MATCHED SOCKS
• SPARE MITTENS
• TOILET PLUNGERS
• REPLACEMENT HAMSTERS
• HOT COFFEE
• WINE COOLERS
• TYLENOL
• RITALIN
• PROZAC
...baby wipes, a princess costume, & a new goldfish please.
MOM MOBILE
©1996 MARGIE CHERRY

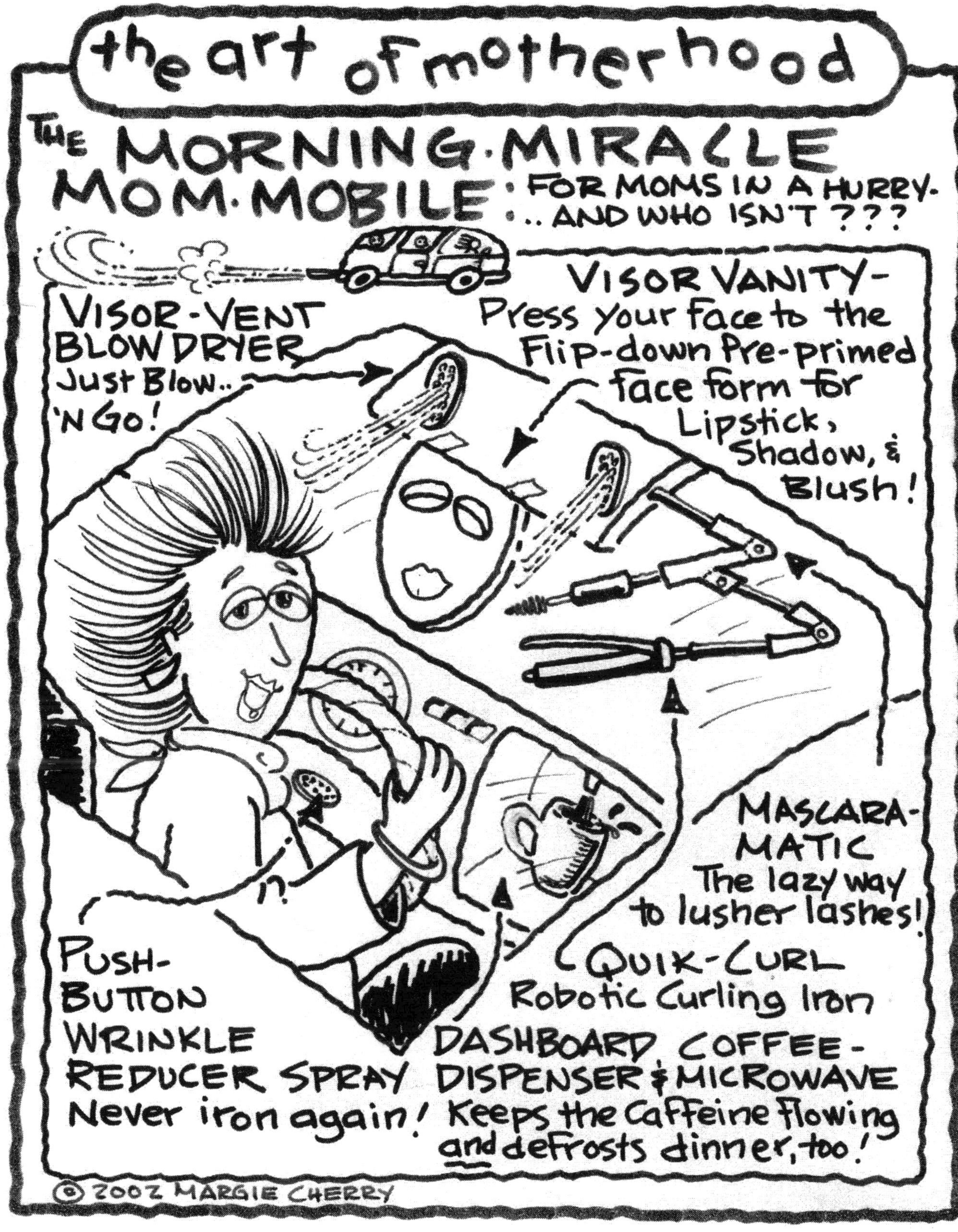
the art of motherhood
THE MORNING · MIRACLE MOM · MOBILE: FOR MOMS IN A HURRY-
.. AND WHO ISN'T ???
VISOR-VENT BLOW DRYER Just Blow.. 'N Go!
VISOR VANITY- Press your face to the Flip-down Pre-primed face form for Lipstick, Shadow, & Blush!
MASCARA-MATIC The lazy way to lusher lashes!
QUIK-CURL Robotic Curling Iron
PUSH-BUTTON WRINKLE REDUCER SPRAY Never iron again!
DASHBOARD COFFEE-DISPENSER & MICROWAVE Keeps the caffeine flowing and defrosts dinner, too!
© 2002 MARGIE CHERRY

# the art of motherhood

## ESSENTIAL MOMMY TOOLS
### THE SWISS MOMMY KNIFE

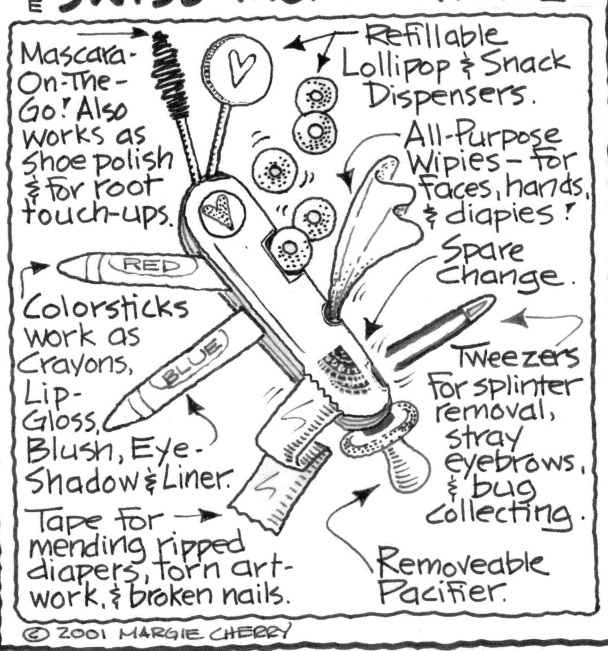

Mascara-On-The-Go! Also works as shoe polish & for root touch-ups.

Refillable Lollipop & Snack Dispensers.

All-Purpose Wipies - for faces, hands, & diapies!

Colorsticks work as Crayons, Lip-Gloss, Blush, Eye-Shadow & Liner.

Spare Change.

Tweezers for splinter removal, stray eyebrows, & bug collecting.

Tape for mending ripped diapers, torn artwork, & broken nails.

Removeable Pacifier.

CIY
Cartoon-It-Yourself

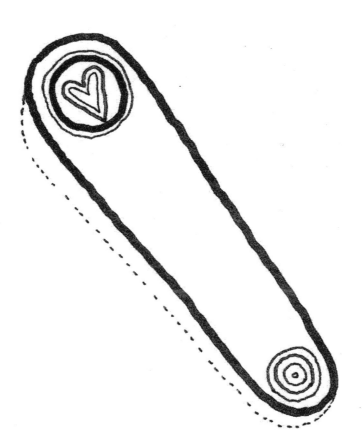

Swiss Mommy Knife

What's on YOUR knife???
Draw your essential tools!!!

# Margie Cherry
## The Original Mom-Commer

Margie Cherry didn't set out to help create a new brand of humor. She set out to save her own sanity, spare her family her neurotic angst, and to kvetch a little to let off steam. So she doodled her anxieties, frustrations, and feelings of maternal failure in a notebook and then tried to persuade greeting card companies to turn her illustrations into a line of cards for overwhelmed moms. Card companies were not interested. It was 1990. Motherhood, of the irreverent kind, was not yet a hot commodity.

♥

Before the internet gave birth to the screaming triplets of Mommy Blogs, Mommy Products and Mommy Culture (and almost before the birth of the internet itself), Margie was giving birth to two daughters and a new kind of humor she dubbed "Mom-Com" first with her groundbreaking cartoon "The Art of Motherhood" then with her stand-up "Momedy" act (which she had to give up because of all the vomiting…on her part as well as the audience's) and lastly with her popular seminars, "Mom's Comedy Workshop" where she taught moms to save their own sanity by creating comedy to deal with the stresses of parenthood. There was considerably less spit-up involved.

♥

By 2004, with her kids nearly grown and therefore less to groan about, she put down her pen and ink and quietly retired from cartooning, having just about broken even with her neighborhood art supply pusher. Although her cartoons were included in four humor anthologies and appeared frequently in the national humor monthly *The Funny Times*, the world never quite took notice of this thing called mom-com.

♥

Five years later there were 23 million moms reading or writing mommy-blogs every week, with advertisers pouring buckets of money into their sticky little peanut-buttered hands. It's one thing to miss the boat. It's another to be at the dock, ready and waiting, before the boat is even built, let alone arrived. It's great to be a pioneer--isn't it?

♥

Margie gave up comedy for career counseling and now finds deep satisfaction in working with clients who do as they're told, rarely sass her in public, and never, ever wipe their snotty little noses on her favorite shirt.

♥

She lives outside of Philadelphia with her husband Ivan Kimmelman, and her cat Sylvie. Her daughters are grown, and she assumes that having made them the subject of her cartoons for most of their early years as she mocked motherhood is the reason they have both moved to Brooklyn. She misses them terribly.

**MargieCherry.com**
**Momedy@MargieCherry.com**

Made in the USA
Columbia, SC
06 December 2017